Machine Vision

Machine Vision

How Algorithms are Changing the Way We See the World

JILL WALKER RETTBERG

polity

First published in 2023 by Polity Press

Polity Press
65 Bridge Street
Cambridge CB2 1UR, UK

Polity Press
111 River Street
Hoboken, NJ 07030, USA

ISBN-13: 978-1-5095-4522-3
ISBN-13: 978-1-5095-4523-0 (pb)

A catalogue record for this book is available from the British Library.

Library of Congress Control Number: 2022948740

Typeset in 11 on 14pt Warnock Pro
by Cheshire Typesetting Ltd, Cuddington, Cheshire
Printed and bound in Great Britain by TJ Books Limited, Padstow, Cornwall

For further information on Polity, visit our website:
politybooks.com

Contents

Acknowledgements

The ideas in this book have grown and developed over many years, and I am indebted to many friends and colleagues for generous discussions and debates. Both the Digital Culture and the Electronic Literature research group at the University of Bergen have been invaluable spaces for sharing and generating ideas. I am grateful for feedback on drafts from my colleagues Gabriele de Seta, Marianne Gunderson, Ragnhild Solberg, Linda Kronman, Joseph Tabbi, Scott Rettberg and Tuva Mossin. Ingunn Lunde generously answered my questions about the meaning of the original Russian title of *Man with a Movie Camera* and helped me catch a couple of embarrassing misspellings too. Annette Markham gave me wonderfully inspiring feedback on an early stage of the draft at our writing retreat just before the pandemic broke out. My editor at Polity, Mary Savigar, gave very useful feedback on drafts of the manuscript, and the peer reviewers' feedback was also very helpful. I also want to thank Stephanie Homer at Polity and Caroline Richmond for copy-editing. My developmental editor, Margaret Puskar-Pasewicz, gave me great feedback especially in the early phases of the project, and for the final spurt I've leaned on my writing group: Laura Saetveit

Miles, Mathilde Sørensen and Sari Pietkäinen. Our writing coach K. Anne Amienne has followed this project from the beginning, when I first realised I could spend project funding on a coach to make sure I do the writing I really want to do.

In Oak Park several people generously shared their thoughts with me and gave me feedback on my analysis of the Flock Safety camera debates. I would particularly like to thank Scott Sakiyama, Kathleen Finn Bell and Alicia Chastain for generously reading and commenting on a draft of the chapter about Oak Park. Thank you also to Emily Bembeneck and Sendhil Mullainathan at the Center for Applied AI at the University of Chicago for inviting me to be a visiting scholar at the center and for their support while I was there.

This book is an outcome of research funded by the European Research Council (ERC) under the European Union's Horizon 2020 research and innovation programme (grant agreement No 771800).

Most of all, thank you to Scott and to Aurora Jonathan, Jesse and Benji. Thank you for letting me see the world with you.

Introduction

Seeing more, seeing differently, seeing everything

Argus was a giant with a hundred eyes, older than the ancient Greek gods but a servant to them. He could see in all directions at once and he never stopped watching. Even when he slept, only some of his eyes were closed.

Human vision is far more limited. We have just two eyes in the front of our heads and can't see what is behind us at all. We see what is straight ahead of us clearly, but our peripheral vision is poor. Many other animals have eyes on the sides or even on the backs of their heads. Some species can see infrared or ultraviolet light. Humans cannot. We can see only in the rather limited way that our eyes, our brains and our bodies enable. And yet, for sighted humans, vision is the primary way we make sense of the world around us.

Humans have used technology to expand our limited vision for millennia. We have imagined mythical creatures such as Argus and created stories about future technologies such as optical implants or holographic phones. The dream and the promise of machine vision is that it will enhance our limited human vision. We imagine that technologies will allow us to see more, to see differently and even to see everything. But each of these new ways of seeing carries with it its own blind spots. The blind spots and distortions of machine vision may be different from the blind spots and distortions of unaided human vision, but machine vision technologies are limited by their own material constraints. Machine vision changes what humans can see. From telescopes and cinematic cameras to facial recognition, smart surveillance and emotion recognition: how will these new extensions of human vision change our perception of the world? What will we *not* see when seeing with machine vision?

This book analyses the relationships between humans and machine vision technologies by exploring the historical development of technologies that have helped us to see, ranging from the first mirror, which was carved from black obsidian 8,000 years ago, through the telescopes that ignited the scientific revolution, to contemporary networks of surveillance cameras that send automated alerts about suspicious activities to their owners or to law enforcement. Machine vision can create great beauty and make wonderful things possible. New visual technologies enable scientific advances and help to cure diseases. Artists and filmmakers use animation, virtual reality and images generated by deep learning to create breath-taking imagined spaces and images.

Machine vision also comes with many problems and limitations. Algorithmic bias affects machine vision as it does other technologies using machine learning and big datasets. Facial recognition systems are often intrinsically biased; they are better at identifying white men than black women. A neural network trained on internet images with English captions will re-create the bias in the training data, generating images and propagating a version of a world where humans are almost always white, nurses are women, doctors are men and terrorists look Arabic.[1]

Some visual technologies, such as microscopes or high-speed cameras, allow us to see objects that are too small, too distant, or too fast for the human eye to detect. Others allow us to see wavelengths beyond visible light, such as night vision goggles using infrared to perceive warm bodies in the dark. We use radar and ultrasound and LIDAR to send out signals that bounce off objects, and that allows us to generate three-dimensional models of objects we cannot otherwise see: approaching aeroplanes in the dark or an unborn child sucking its thumb in its mother's womb. Satellites, drones and networks of surveillance cameras create vast datasets of images that can be processed by computers to find and identify individuals or track changes in ways that were never before possible. Cameras keep watch for us, fastened to doorbells, street signs and buildings. These cameras are automated by artificial intelligence models that recognise faces or car licence plates, sending alerts to their owners or the police when they identify something as suspicious.

I define machine vision as the registration, analysis and representation of visual information by machines and algorithms. Machine vision technologies register visual information and store it as data that can be processed computationally. My definition is intentionally broad to allow us to analyse the larger-scale shifts that are currently taking place in visual representation. I chose the term 'machine vision' instead of 'computer vision' because I want to include the history of seeing with technologies. New visual technologies have been agents of cultural change well before computers. As I'll discuss in chapter 1, the fifteenth-century invention of linear perspective, coupled with the glass lenses needed for telescopes, were central to the scientific revolution and the modern age. Photography, cinema and other nineteenth- and twentieth-century imaging technologies likewise came with societal change and scientific advances. Machine vision has advanced exponentially in the last decade due to AI: there has been rapid progress in machine learning models trained on massive datasets. Will these new technologies lead to new paradigms, as happened with telescopes in the Renaissance and photography in the nineteenth century? This book aims to contribute to our understanding of what we are becoming.

The idea of artificial intelligence (AI) is at least as old as the ancient Greeks, as Adrienne Meyor demonstrates in her book *Gods and Robots*, but it was in the 1950s that advances in computer science made actual thinking machines begin to seem feasible. Let me try to explain how the AI used to generate images or recognise faces works. Two main strands of AI have been developed from the 1950s.[2] The first, symbolic AI, is based on the idea that a form of common sense could be explicitly coded as a set of rules or algorithms that would allow a computer to think rationally. The second kind, sub-symbolic AI, is based on machine learning from data. With machine learning, a computer program is written to analyse a dataset and infer its own rules from patterns it finds in the data. Until the 1990s, symbolic AI seemed the most likely to succeed. However, with the extreme expansion of available training data due to internet content, along with increased processing power, subsymbolic AI or machine learning took off. This led to radical improvements first in machine vision and soon after in large language models that can generate news stories, summarise texts or act as a very convincing conversation partner.[3] Current AI is impressive, but it can still only do specific tasks, such as classifying images, playing a game of chess or generating text that looks similar to something a human might write. Some people think that in time this will lead to artificial general intelligence (AGI) – that is, a computational system that, like humans, can do many different tasks and that might even be sentient. I love reading science fiction about sentient AI, but I think this is still firmly fiction. In chapter 2 I'll discuss how AI can be said to *cognise* rather than think in a self-reflective way as humans do. The way AI cognises is quite different from human cognition, and that means that AI-driven machine vision is quite different from human vision.

Machine learning was first used in image recognition. In 1957, Frank Rosenblatt proposed 'the perceptron', a single-layer neural network that could read handwritten numbers.[4] In this kind of machine learning, individual units ('neurons') are trained on a set of images labelled by humans. For instance, an image of a cat is labelled 'cat' and an image of a dog is labelled 'dog'. The units are given random numeric values to start with and the program adjusts their values based on the input. The input from all values is then combined and checked against the label. Imagine that the correct value for 'cat' is 1 and 'not cat' is 0, and the first round of training produces the score 0.6. The model is now given the information that the image is a cat and the value should be 1. Then it goes through the data again, changing its processes more or less at random. If the score after the second round is closer to 1, the model learns that, whatever its new strategies were, they were better. It tries again, becoming less random with each round as it learns which strategies are successful and which are not. After many such rounds, the model will be trained and able to identify the image of a cat that it was trained on. But it may not be able to identify a photo of a new cat.

In the 1970s, deep learning was proposed, where there are several layers of 'neurons', each layer feeding its results to the next. Deep learning produced better results than Rosenblatt's single-layer neural network but was not as successful as symbolic AI and was not developed much further until the 1990s.[5] A major shift occurred in 2010, when researchers gained access to big data generated on the internet and to far higher computing power. Deep learning (also often called 'neural networks') made rapid advances, driven first by image recognition trained on ImageNet, a database of images scraped from the internet that was semantically organised using WordNet. Kate Crawford and Trevor Paglen's artwork *ImageNet Roulette* and their accompanying essay explain how this works and demonstrate how problematic the results can be. WordNet includes categories that cannot be unambiguously expressed in images (such as 'sex worker') as well as slurs and other problematic terms, so when used to classify images, and especially images of people, you run into problems.[6] Rapid advances were also occurring in large language models (LLMs), which are trained on vast amounts of writing from the web and from books. By 2017, both text generation and image recognition gave impressive results.[7] Self-supervised learning also came to the fore, meaning that datasets no longer have to be annotated by humans before being used as training data for a machine learning model.

In 2021, a group of Stanford researchers coined the term 'foundation model' to describe models that use deep learning at such scale that they gain new capabilities, in particular *homogenisation* and *emergence*.[8] They have a homogenising effect because one model is used for many tasks, which can give more stability but also means any defect or bias will be inherited by all downstream applications. Emergence is another key feature: these models have unanticipated effects. For instance, the developers did not expect that large language models would be able to generate text. Foundation models are so expensive to train that, as of 2022, only big tech companies can afford to train them, but they are then fine-tuned and put to many other downstream uses.

As I finish writing this book, image generation models such as DALL-E, Midjourney and Stable Diffusion are capable of generating photorealistic images from written prompts, and large language models such as GTP-4 can have convincing conversations and answer general knowledge questions, though still with some factual errors. These models depend upon the deep-learning structure I described above, but they are trained on even more data and with even more parameters. In my simple example above, where 'cat' is 1 and 'not cat' is 0, there is just one parameter – cat or not cat. Current models can be trained on more than a billion parameters. To an AI model, that cat is understood as a vector – that is, a list of numeric values, one for each parameter. Perhaps the vector for cat is [0.642, 0.231, 0.932, . . .], and so on. Once trained, the model no longer has access to the original photos. Instead it operates with what is called a *vector space* or *semantic space*, or sometimes just *space*, where all the vectors are organised in a multidimensional grid. Remember those coordinate grids you draw in seventh grade, where you plot a point on an x–y grid? To find the point [1,4] you draw a line from 1 on the x-axis and 4 on the y-axis and see where the lines meet. The vector space or semantic space of a machine learning model is like that, but each parameter is an axis. There isn't just an x-axis and a y-axis, but a z-axis and a billion more dimensions. I doubt you can imagine that visually, but powerful computers can compute it.[9] *Latent space* is another term that is used in machine learning research: this is a lower-dimension version of the vector space that can be sufficient to generate new data that is similar to the training data. The important thing to remember is that a trained deep-learning model does not directly access the training data; it accesses only this multidimensional set of vectors describing different features of the dataset, such as words or concepts or characteristics of images.

Image generation models such as DALL-E are trained on images with captions from the web.[10] Users can write a prompt describing an image, and the model will generate images based on the concepts it has learned from the dataset. These concepts can be surprisingly complex. For example, OpenAI's CLIP model has a specific neuron (or unit) that has learned to respond to the concept 'spider' and can use it to group drawings of spiders, the written word 'spider' and pictures of Spiderman. Reading the paper announcing these 'multimodal neurons', you can sense the wonder of the researchers, who describe such a model almost as though it is a child: 'Some neurons seem like topics out of a kindergarten curriculum: weather, seasons, letters, counting, or primary colors. All of these features, even the trivial-seeming ones, have rich multimodality, such as a yellow neuron firing for images of the words "yellow", "banana" and "lemon", in addition to the color.'[11] The paper, which is rich with interactive visualisations, goes on to show how emotions such as 'happy' or 'sleepy' can be identified across facial expressions or body language, and how concepts can also connect to their opposites.

If you would like a deeper understanding of the technical aspects of AI that contemporary machine vision builds upon, I recommend Melanie Mitchell's book *Artificial Intelligence* and Kate Crawford's *Atlas of AI*.[12] Both of these books give solid but accessible explanations for a general audience. The first few pages of the Stanford report on foundation models also provide a brief but relatively accessible technical explanation. Mark Andrejevic and Neil Selwyn's book *Facial Recognition* details the historical development of facial recognition in particular and explains how this specific technology works in more detail than I can here. OpenAI, Meta and Google also provide accessible explanations to many of their models on their websites. These often include interactive visuals, as well as links to the research papers describing each model.

The focus of this book is how different kinds of machine vision allow humans to see in new ways. Without technology, human vision is situated in two eyes and a brain that processes their visual input. With access to home surveillance cameras and DALL-E and satellite images of my neighbourhood, I can see a lot more than just what is straight in front of me.

How vision is situated

The chapters of this book will explore ways in which machine vision expands or escapes the situatedness of human vision:

by seeing more, by seeing differently, by seeing everything, by being seen and, finally, by exploring what machine vision does *not* see.

Vision is always situated. I use 'situated' in a sense established by Donna Haraway in her influential article 'Situated knowledges', which was published in 1988. Haraway argues that the closest we can get to objective knowledge is to acknowledge that we always have only a partial perspective. Visual technologies, from satellite surveillance to medical imaging, seem to promise the impossible: 'the god trick of seeing everything from nowhere', as Haraway writes.[13] In contrast to this 'god trick', Haraway argues that knowledge is embodied. Therefore 'objectivity turns out to be about particular and specific embodiment.'[14] When I write that vision is situated, I mean that we always see from our own situation in the world, from a particular standpoint and within the limitations of the physical constraints of our bodies. When I look out of my window, I see a view of my neighbourhood that is slightly different from what a neighbour would see from their window, and quite different from what a satellite image of the neighbourhood would capture. What I see is also situated by how sharp my vision is, by my personal experiences (do I know who lives in each building or what it means that my neighbour hasn't put the trash out as they usually do), by the time and season (is it dark or light), and many other things.

Machine vision technologies often present dazzling overviews that appear to escape this situatedness: satellite images showing the globe in amazing detail, images of distant galaxies or of the microscopic worlds inside the cells of our bodies. These kinds of image appear to be able to show the world as though we are outside of it. They appear to be objective and to show the world as it really is. Haraway argues, and I agree with her, that this objective outside view is impossible.

Saying that vision is situated also means that seeing is embodied. What we can see is shaped by the constraints of our bodies or by the constraints of the technologies we see with. We see with two eyes, not a hundred, and, unlike many species, we have poor peripheral vision. I'll return to how different species and different technologies see differently in chapter 2.

When we use machine vision we are no longer entirely bound to our human point of view or to the limitations and affordances of our eyes and our brains. We can see the Earth from outer space, or the blood vessels inside our bodies; we can see the heat of bodies 30 kilometres away[15] or capture the motion of a galloping horse in a high-speed photograph, where we would otherwise see nothing but a blur. Machine vision can make distant events feel very close, as when we see live videos of war atrocities, a carjacking captured by a neighbour's doorbell camera, or TikTok videos recorded in a teenager's bedroom. New visual technologies such as searchable satellite images and electron microscopes and VR glasses are all situated and thus limited ways of seeing, but we easily forget this. It is easy to be swept away by the promotional material and the gorgeous visuals. Perhaps we are also a little seduced by Haraway's 'god trick', or what José van Dijck calls *dataism*: 'the ideology of dataism shows characteristics of a widespread belief in the objective quantification and potential tracking of all kinds of human behavior and sociality through online media technologies.'[16] This trust in technology as an almost divine power will be a recurring theme in this book.

Machine vision is non-human in that it allows us humans to see things that would otherwise be invisible to us. At the same time machine vision is completely human: humans imagine it, humans design it and humans use it. Machines do not see without us, or, perhaps more precisely, they would not see without us. Machines depend on humans as much as humans depend on machines. Machine vision doesn't 'see' alone. Rather, its sensory apparatus – its hardware and the algorithms it uses to process data – is always part of an assemblage that humans also participate in.

I understand machine vision technologies not as technological monoliths that inevitably determine human behaviour but as participants in assemblages where humans, technologies and cultural contexts act together. By focusing on the assemblage more than on the technology itself, I build upon posthumanist and feminist theories that emphasise relationships between humans and non-human agents such as technologies, institutions and our natural environment. The prefix *post* in posthumanism indicates that it comes *after* the humanism that began in the Enlightenment era, when the human was seen as the centre of the universe, the subject who could rule and control all other creatures and entities. For this master human subject, technology, the environment and even other groups of humans were seen primarily as objects or tools. Posthumanism emphasises relationships and mutual interconnection instead of the binary opposition between an active subject and a passive object. The concept of the assemblage helps us see how different agents come together in different constellations in different contexts.

We don't fully control the technologies we use, and the technologies don't fully control us. By being aware of the assemblages we choose to enter into (or that are thrust upon us) we can start to untangle how technologies work in specific contexts. Then we can try to design assemblages that help build the kinds of communities and societies we want to live in. To understand technology, then, we also need to understand the assemblages it participates in. I'll go into more detail in chapter 2 about what it means to use the concept of assemblages to think about technology.

The assemblages don't consist only of humans and machines; cultural and regulatory contexts are also important. This book was written partly in Norway, my usual home, and partly in the USA, my temporary home for the first half of 2022. The contrasts between the two countries seemed stronger this time than on my previous visits, with anxiety ratcheted sky high in the USA due to the pandemic, to rising crime rates and to political tensions. The more I learned about how technologies are discussed and used in the Chicago suburb where I was living, the more I realised how differently these technologies were being adopted and understood there compared to my own home environment in Norway.

Technology does not have the same effects in all contexts. The mere existence of surveillance technologies such as automated licence plate readers or facial recognition does not necessarily mean all the world will use them or that they will be used in the same way in every context. Even within one country different technologies can be regulated or viewed very differently. In the USA, it is far easier to install facial recognition cameras in a school than to ban guns. Local US police departments can combine data from licence plate readers with hundreds of other public and data sources with little regulation, but there are no central gun registries. That information is protected by strong political lobbies.[17] This means that it is far easier to implement smart surveillance systems across the USA than it would be to change gun control laws. In Norway, the private smart surveillance systems that have spread across the USA are for the most part illegal because of strong privacy legislation. These political and institutional structures are also important participants in the assemblages machine vision enters into.

Situations and stories as analytical tools

One method I use to analyse the relationship between humans and machine vision technologies is exploring specific examples of situations where humans and technologies act together. Some of these machine vision situations are fictional or imagined and some are real.

The term 'machine vision situation' comes from my work with a stellar group of researchers on a digital humanities project to create a database documenting how machine vision technologies are represented in digital art, video games and narratives such as movies and novels.[18] We wanted to explore how humans and machine vision technologies interact in assemblages where agency is distributed rather than framing the human as using technology as a tool. Working as a team, Ragnhild Solberg, Marianne Gunderson, Linda Kronman and I developed a model for analysing situations in the artworks, games and narratives that involved machine vision technologies. We identified agents in each situation and described actions they took in a structured way, so we could use data analysis and data visualisations to see overall patterns across the 500 novels, movies, video games and artworks we analysed. We discussed and wrote about our interpretations of how machine vision was used and represented in individual works, too, and discussed real-world examples with input from our collaborator Gabriele de Seta.[19]

Spending so much time reading, playing, watching and analysing art, games and narratives about machine vision gave us a very broad overview of how machine vision technologies are portrayed in fiction and art. In this book I draw upon many examples from these works, especially from science fiction literature and film. Throughout you will find short readings of artworks, movies, games and novels where machine vision technologies are central. I interlace the more theoretical discussions with these analyses of fiction because fiction allows for another mode of understanding new technology that enables a more emotional and often more visceral, embodied kind of insight. You have probably noticed the surge in the popularity of science fiction in recent years. The most popular science fiction today deals with the near future. Series such as *Black Mirror* exaggerate contemporary issues just a little bit to make the ethical dilemmas even more acute: what happens when everyone has an implant that records everything they see or hear, as in 'The entire history of you', or when a mother implants her child with the Arkangel system, allowing the mother both to see everything the child sees and to alter the child's sight so that 'inappropriate content', such as blood, is filtered out and not seen by the child.[20]

Artists are also exploring machine vision, both as spectacle and in more critical ways. Refik Anadol's gorgeous, crowd-pleasing *Machine Hallucination* installations use neural networks trained on thousands of images of cities to generate videos showing new, dream-like skyscrapers rising and falling, like the cities we know but strange. Other artists use machine vision technologies for critique and exploration of new situations that may become common. For instance, Lauren McCarthy and Kyle McDonald's artwork *US+* is a plug-in to be used during video chats that analyses users' facial expressions and gives live advice about how to improve their interpersonal relationship. Video games are another popular medium where explorations of machine vision are common, whether as a playful aspect of the interface, as in the augmented reality of *Pokémon GO*, or as a substantial element in the story. The *Watch Dog* games let players view and control the game world through surveillance systems,[21] while an indie game such as Samantha Gorman's *Tendar* lets players adopt a virtual guppie that must be fed with emotions that it harvests from the player's smile using emotion recognition algorithms.[22]

Watching movies, playing games, reading novels and experiencing artworks are important ways in which people think through possible situations that may occur with new technologies such as machine vision. The imaginary worlds of stories, games and art allow us to explore an emotional engagement with new technologies and the possible societal and ethical changes that may come with them. This emotional engagement tends to be lacking from computer science textbooks or patents for new smart home technologies. Through empathy with characters in fictional situations, we imagine how we ourselves would react and what choices we would make. By interacting with games and digital artworks, we can make choices without the consequences of real life. The affective relationship we have with art, stories and games lets us explore a sensory knowledge and develop our sense of what technologies might lead to and what technologies would be good for us – or not so good.

To understand how machine vision is affecting the way we humans see and relate to the world around us, we need to understand the relationships between humans and technologies. A few years ago, I proposed situated data analysis as a method for understanding how data is used and presented on various platforms. Situated data analysis explores how the same data is framed – or situated – in different ways for different audiences and purposes.[23] It is about following the data, and machine vision converts the visual to data. A situated data analysis could be a useful method for examining how data from automated licence plate readers, for instance, is presented to police and processed in different situations, ranging from alerts received by officers, to dashboards the police department can use to analyse traffic flow, to the predictive policing algorithms that the data can feed into. In this book, however, I am interested less in the data itself and more in how we humans are affected by machines and in the technologies that sense and process the data. Focusing on stories, situations, assemblages and emotions allows me to bring that affect and those relationships into my analysis.

Representational and operational images

Human sight is the ability to perceive and interpret electromagnetic radiation, or light, in the visible spectrum. Our eyes and brains sense and process the light in our surroundings to create an image of the world that we use to orient ourselves. Machine vision technologies can also sense light, but they do not need to convert it into an image. They process light as data.

Humans interpret different wavelengths of light as having different colours. Having input from two separate eyes, our brains interpret our stereoscopic vision as information about depth and distance. A self-driving car senses a lot of the same data about the environment as we do, in addition to other data such as GPS locations from satellites and data from the car and its engine. But there is no need for the computer to convert the data it gathers into a visual image, a two-dimensional representation of visual data. Instead, it processes the zeros and ones of its machine-readable data to calculate how it should respond to its surroundings. If we can even call this an image, it is a very different kind of image to the ones we are used to seeing in art museums, on the front of magazines or in YouTube videos and Instagram feeds. The car may well represent the data in visual form on a screen for the driver or passengers to see, but this representation is not necessary for the car to function.

A useful distinction can be made here between *representational* images, where the main point of the image is to *show* something, and *operational* images, where the main point is to *do* something. A snapshot from a family holiday or a painting on a gallery wall is a representation, whereas the images captured by the camera of a self-driving car are operational.

The term *operative image* was coined by the filmmaker Harun Farocki in 2001 in connection with his artwork *Eye/ Machine*. In 2004 he defined the term more explicitly: operative images 'are images that do not represent an object, but rather are part of an operation.' In 2014, the artist Trevor Paglen developed the idea further:

> [T]he machines were starting to see for themselves. Harun Farocki was one of the first to notice that image-making machines and algorithms were poised to inaugurate a new visual regime. Instead of simply representing things in the world, the machines and their images were starting to 'do' things in the world.[24]

In practice, many images are both representational and operational. For instance, passport photographs have been used for more than a century as a means of verifying the bearer's identity and are representations of the bearer's face. With electronic processing of passports, the photos are also stored in databases where they can be processed and used for automatic identity verification. There is still a photograph representing your face in your passport, but more important is the digitally stored information about your face that is processed by a computer and compared to the data captured by the camera as you stand waiting for the gate to open. This digitally processed photograph is *operational*.

The 'operational images' that are generated and processed by the autonomous car or the passport gates at the airport, or by any number of other machines, are clearly not representational in the sense that the *Mona Lisa* or a movie are representations. But they are still constructed. The very act of deciding which data to collect shapes that data. The original 'Blue Marble' image, the photograph of the earth as seen from space, first released by NASA in 1972, was a snapshot captured on an analogue camera by an astronaut. But, as Laura Kurgan discussed in her book *Close Up at a Distance*, newer 'photographs' of the Earth as seen from space are the product of data processing rather than the capture of light that we know from analogue or optical photography. In these photorealistic images of an Earth with no cloud cover and perfect lighting, there is no direct relationship between what we see in the images produced by machine vision and the real world. It's a 'god trick', as Haraway would say. Truth in such images is no longer a question of 'seeing is believing'. Instead, as Laura Kurgan wrote, truth 'is intimately related to resolution, to measurability, to the construction of a reliable algorithm for translating between representation and reality.'[25]

Once we realise that images aren't just representational, we can begin to think more about what else images can *do*. If we

understand 'operative images' as images that contain data and
instructions for using that data, maybe we could say that all
images are operative: they encode visual information in a way
that can be processed by our eyes and brains and interpreted as
a representation of something actual or imagined. Abstract art
and architecture can cause us to feel in certain ways. We can
also think of diagrams, maps and visualisations as operative
images.

Carolyn L. Kane sees the decline of representational
images as such a fundamental aspect of today's society that
she calls our time *post-optical*, arguing that we no longer
use sight and visual elements as ends in themselves but as
means to another end.[26] Kane is particularly interested in
colour, and she gives the example of chromakey video, where
producers use a blue or green background – not because it
will look good in the final image but so that the colour will
'negate itself', as Kane writes: the blue or green pixels will
be replaced by another background image. In brain imaging,
synthetic fluorescent proteins are inserted so that the final
image can display the colourful flows to map brain function.
Colour used to give us information to help us interpret our
surroundings, but its function has changed: 'Color is not
exclusively about vision', as Kane writes. 'Rather, it is a system
of control used to manage and discipline perception and
thus reality.'

Kane's term 'post-optical' is a nod to Friedrich Kittler's
monumental book *Optical Media*, a book composed of
lectures he gave in 1999 on the material and technological
development of media. Optical media, in Kittler's framework,
are media that can be seen and interpreted by the human eye
at any point. Kittler never uses the term 'post-optical', but he
describes the concept in his discussion of electronic media
such as television: 'In contrast to film, television was already
no longer optics. It is possible to hold a film reel up to the sun
and see what every frame shows. It is possible to intercept

television signals, but not to look at them, because they only exist as electronic signals.'[27]

Contemporary machine vision is certainly post-optical in this sense. The computationally processed sensor data that allows a self-driving car to navigate is not something we can look at or perceive in any straightforward manner. When an AI model trained on hundreds of thousands of images classifies new images, it calculates statistical probabilities that an image represents a specific object. It doesn't produce explanations why.

This book builds upon the work of many other scholars. There are excellent books on specific machine vision technologies, such as Mark Andrejevic and Neil Selwyn's *Facial Recognition* and Graham Meikle's *Deepfakes*, or Lila Lee-Morrison's *Portraits of Automated Facial Recognition: On Machinic Ways of Seeing the Face*. Anthony McCosker and Rowan Wilken's *Automating Vision: The Social Implications of the New Camera Consciousness* explores the social impact of smart cameras across domains ranging from surveillance and facial recognition to drones and self-driving cars. Other books focus on specific uses of technologies, such as Thomas Stubblefield's art history take in *Drone Art: The Everywhere War as Medium*, Julia Hildebrand's analysis of drones as a mobile medium in *Aerial Play: Drone Medium, Mobility, Communication, and Culture* or Arthur Michel's popular science account of satellite surveillance in *Eyes in the Sky: The Secret Rise of Gorgon Stare and How it Will Watch Us All*. My own book *Seeing Ourselves through Technology* discussed selfies and how we use technologies to see ourselves and shape our ideas of who we are and want to be. Simone Browne's *Dark Matters: On the Surveillance of Blackness* shows how slavery and surveillance are interlinked and how biometrics and machine vision today still embed this racial violence. Kelly Gates's 2011 book *Our Biometric Future* was an early analysis of facial recognition and other biometric technologies that remains useful. I have been inspired by the connections Anne Friedberg made between linear perspective and twenty-first-century visual technology in her 2006 book *The Virtual Window: From Alberti to Microsoft*. I discuss books written before digital technology was prevalent, such as Vilém Flusser's books on photography and Friedrich Kittler's *Optical Media*. I also build on N. Katherine Hayles's work analysing how computers are *cognisers*, as well as her writing on cyber-semiotics that begins to explore how machines sense and make sense of the world.

Structure of the book

Chapter 1 is about how we use technology to see *more* than we can see with our own eyes. It starts with the first known visual technology to be created by humans: an 8,000-year-old polished stone mirror designed to be held in a hand. The chapter follows the thread through glass lenses and telescopes to photography and technologies that allow us to observe waves that are outside the spectrum that is visible to humans, such as x-rays, infrared, ultrasound or gravitational waves. The main argument in this chapter is that the desire to see *more* generally situates technology as a tool that can expand humans' access to the world. We assume that we are in charge, and that these technologies augment our abilities without really altering us. However, by examining these technologies in detail, I show how human agency is far more entwined with our technologies than we may imagine. These technologies are more than just tools; they affect us.

Chapter 2 explores how we use technology to see *differently*. How do machines perceive the world? I analyse two twentieth-century cases where the camera is framed as autonomous and of seeing differently to humans: the early Soviet Kinoks collective's *kino-eye* and Vilém Flusser's theory of the camera that programs the human operator. Following N. Katherine Hayles,

I use biosemiotics to better understand how humans and other animals see in situated and specific ways and cybersemiotics to think about how machines sense the world.

Chapter 3 is about the human dream of being able to see *everything*. I explore this dream of omnivoyance through a case study: the debate about the implementation of automated licence plate readers in Oak Park, a neighbourhood just outside Chicago's city limits. The chapter analyses how the rapid introduction of automated surveillance cameras in the United States is deeply embedded in local contexts such as the history of the community, local politics, perceptions of safety and community support, and fear. Machine vision is situated not just in the materiality of the technology but also in the assemblages of which it is part.

Chapter 4 is about *being seen* and how machine vision sees us. I explore the algorithmic gaze of machine vision watching humans through three case studies. First, I discuss selfie filters and the ways biometrics and facial recognition algorithms conceive of human faces, framing facial recognition and emotion recognition as having a *normalising* gaze. My second case study explores how machine vision is used to automate grocery shopping, library access and other interactions that previously required us to collaborate with other humans. Finally, I explore a fictional example of a benevolent AI dictator, Thunderhead, from Neal Shusterman's young adult series of novels *The Arc of the Scythe*. These analyses of how we are seen by machine vision also deepen my argument that it is the assemblage as a whole that sees, not the technology alone.

Chapter 5 is about the blind spots of machine vision and how in many cases it sees *less* than humans. This chapter discusses the figure of the trickster hero in stories who fools and evades machine vision and of the rebel who fights and refuses it. I consider folk theories about how image recognition works and how to evade it, together with adversarial techniques that make deep-learning algorithms fail to recognise an image, ranging from artist and activist projects to computer science strategies. I also examine how human bodies are made more legible to machines and the dangers of governing through data in this way.

The conclusion is titled 'Hope'. Despite the fear and anxiety in chapter 3 and the oppression in chapter 5, I want to hold on to what gives me hope for the future. The many stories of tricksters and rebels give me hope, as do the playful and artistic experiments that explore how we can see the world in new ways.

To conclude this introduction, I want to say that my words in this book are situated in my personal and professional experience and knowledge, which is partial and limited like everybody else's. This limitation is often a strength, because I am able to analyse specific machine vision situations such as smart surveillance in an American neighbourhood as an outsider who becomes more and more a part of the situation. But there are also many situations of which I have no knowledge. I am a cis, heterosexual white woman who grew up in Australia and Norway speaking English and Norwegian. I studied in Norway and have worked as a researcher and teacher in universities in Norway and the United States. I know far more about European and Anglo-American-Australian cultural history than any other traditions. In this book I have tried to be aware of this rather than taking it for granted, and to seek out diversity when possible.

I should also note that I use 'we' quite often. I want to write conversationally and to speak directly to you, the person reading this book. Often the 'we' in this book refers to you and me: the reader and writer. You and I are both moving through these words, but of course our experiences are not the same, neither of the words in this book nor of the world in general. The pronoun 'we' can be dangerous – it's easy to assume that I am part of a universal 'we' and that everyone in that 'we' experiences the world as I do. The universal 'we' can be oppressive.

It might appear to be the opposite of the situated knowledge I want to share. But 'we' can also be open and fluid. In chapter 2 I analyse a manifesto written by the Soviet filmmaker collective the Kinoks, where the 'we' and the 'I' that narrate the text slip between many meanings: one human, many humans, the humans and machines, perhaps the machines alone. We-narratives – that is, stories told in the first-person plural – have received more and more attention in literary studies in recent years.[28] I think the reason for this is our growing sense that we are not primarily autonomous individuals but participants in networks, assemblages that shift and change. In this book, 'we' sometimes means you and I, sometimes a group of humans, sometimes humans and machines together. Sometimes you won't feel part of my 'we', and that's OK. 'We' emphasises the relationships between us. When I use 'we', please think of it as an invitation, as a touch of companionship, not as a brute force tool claiming everyone is the same.

Finally, I am situated as a human being. Readers of a draft of this manuscript commented that it seemed quite human-centric for a book about assemblages that uses posthumanist theory and aims to avoid thinking of humans as humanist master subjects using technologies as objects and tools. It's true: I write about how humans use technology to see more, to see differently. While I do think it's important to de-centre the human and to acknowledge that we are just one of many species, I can't help but see the world through human eyes, although I also see with technology. Being part of an assemblage doesn't mean I am no longer also myself. Being part of an assemblage means that I am bound to others, that I influence and am influenced by others. So, yes, this book is human-centric in that it is written by a human for other humans. It will no doubt also be used as training data for future machine learning models, so read by machines, but the 'you' in my mind when I write is a human reader, not an AI. Similarly to the way I use *we* to emphasise the relationship between you and me, I try in this book to emphasise the relationship between us humans and the technologies we use. Most importantly, I want to see technology not as an object that can be studied in isolation but as something that does different things in different assemblages. I'll be returning to this point throughout the book.

1

Seeing More:
Histories of Augmenting
Human Vision

The first visual technologies were fire, water and stone. Fire allowed early humans to create light in darkness for the first time, so they could see in the dark. Still water in ponds and bowls provided a reflecting surface with which our ancestors could see themselves. Thousands of years later, the natural mirror of water was supplemented by mirrors of polished stone. The first mirror we know of that was manufactured rather than found was made of polished obsidian in Anatolia (now in Turkey) 8,000 years ago.[1] It is shaped like a half sphere and sized so it can be held in a hand, and it has been polished so brightly that it reflects a face quite superbly.

Technology has been used for millennia, then, to help us to *see more*. Humans cannot see well in the dark, so we light up our surroundings with fire or electricity, or we design night-vision goggles and infrared detectors to augment our vision. Humans cannot see our own faces, so we look into ponds, we polish stone. We use glass and silver to make mirrors. We use smartphones with front-facing cameras to take selfies and employ selfie lenses and filters to see what our faces would look like if we were older or younger or more beautiful, or if we had dog's ears and a tongue.

Seeing more also means capturing that which we see. From cave paintings to cinema, humans have developed ways to record the visual. Over time we have devised how to record the visual more precisely, to see more detail or to see things we cannot see with our own eyes. For instance, humans perceive flickering that is faster than fifty light pulses per second as continuous movement, whereas a machine, or for that matter a bird, can distinguish individual pulses at a much higher frequency. A bird can clearly see the exact movements of a horse's legs when it gallops.[2] Those galloping legs appear as a blur to us humans, or, rather, they were a blur to us until they were captured perfectly by the first high-speed cameras. I'll return to how those photos changed our perception soon.

This chapter is about how humans interact with technology to see *more*. I begin with ancient histories of the first lenses used for magnification and then move to Renaissance histories of camera obscuras and linear perspective, because these led to the development of telescopes, cameras and the very idea that objective visual representations of the world might be possible. These forms of machine vision aim primarily to augment and improve human vision, to *see more*, without fundamentally altering the way we see. These technologies are typically framed as tools, but I argue that, even with these relatively simple and pre-algorithmic machine vision technologies, there is an intertwining of human–machine assemblages.

You may be wondering what ancient mirrors and prisms have to do with the images generated by twenty-first-century deep-learning algorithms. I think they are a necessary foundation for understanding how we interact with technology today. Obviously the technology of polished stone or glass, or even nineteenth-century photography, is very different from the neural networks of our time. But to understand how automated machine vision works today, we need to understand the relationships between humans and these earlier technologies. Looking back at the long history of human–technology relationships allows us to better understand the shifting roles of humans and technologies and to see how machine vision technologies are part of assemblages. Understanding differences over time and across cultures also helps us understand today's technology.

Machine vision is about more than technology: it is an assemblage of human bodies, human culture and technology. Human bodies and eyes share a basic anatomy that we need to consider when analysing how humans see with machine vision. The cultural context is also important in the assemblage into which a specific human or group of humans enters with a specific machine vision technology. The technology is also important, of course, whether it is a polished stone mirror or the algorithms that enhance the selfies you take on your smartphone. In this chapter, I want to show you how thinking about the stone mirror helps us understand the algorithms.

The relationship between humans and technology

The 8,000-year-old obsidian mirror was carved into a half-sphere that comfortably fits in a human hand. Imagine holding that ancient mirror 8,000 years ago. Imagine you have never seen your own face, not in a mirror, not in a photograph. You would hold the stone in your hand, look into its polished surface and see your own face reflected in it as you had never before seen yourself. Today we hold our smartphones in much the same way to take a selfie or video chat with a friend.

Humans have a very close relationship to technology, and a very embodied relationship. We hold the mirror, the phone, up to our faces and we see ourselves. It is easy to think of technology as a tool, as something that we look at or look through. I find it more useful to think of technology as a companion,[3] as something that has an agency of a kind. When we use technology we enter into a relationship with it. That relationship affects us, it affects the technology, and it affects the people and environment around us.

When a person picked up that mirror 8,000 years ago and looked at their reflection in it, they became part of an assemblage consisting of the mirror, the person looking into it, and the people around who were commenting on it: laughing or maybe gasping in awe. It is easy to imagine the mirror being passed around a group, or perhaps being treated as something sacred or special, requiring rituals and careful handling. The weight of the stone would also influence the ways a person could use the mirror.

When I pick up my smartphone to make a TikTok video using a nifty filter, I enter into an assemblage consisting of myself, my phone, and the algorithm that alters my face. We could go further, as Jane Bennett does when analysing the assemblage that makes up the electrical grid in the USA,[4] and include the company that owns TikTok, people who will see my video, and participants in the production chain that built my phone and mined the rare minerals required for its battery. Perhaps we should even include the laws that regulate its use. To understand how we see with machine vision, we need to understand the whole assemblage.

Understanding relationships between humans and technologies as assemblages between human and non-human agents is common in contemporary critical theory. It can be traced back to Deleuze and Guattari's work in the 1980s and 1990s and was developed in a more structured way in actor-network theory in the early 1990s by STS (science and technology studies) scholars such as Madeleine Akrich, Bruno Latour and John Law. Actor-network theory was, among other things, a response to the 'technological determinism' of many scholars, ranging from the mid-twentieth-century Frankfurt School to 1970s apparatus theory in cinema studies or to North American media ecologists in the 1960s, 1970s and 1980s.

One of the most cited examples of technological determinism comes from Lynn White's book *Medieval Technology and Social Change*, published in 1962. White, who was a historian of technology, argued that feudalism was made possible because of the invention of the stirrup. The argument went like this: stirrups allowed the use of horses in battle. Mounted soldiers win battles against foot soldiers, but it is far more expensive to maintain a mounted army. Therefore the rich, who could afford to keep and train soldiers who fought on horseback, won more battles and gained more power. This led to the social structure of feudalism.[5]

Media ecologists such as Marshall McLuhan, Harold Innis and Neil Postman have also been described as technological determinists. Postman, who coined the term media ecology in 1970,[6] saw media as an environment that structures our experiences, while McLuhan saw media as a prosthesis: not a simple tool we can pick up and use, but an extension of the human (or, in his mid-twentieth-century thinking, of *man*) that changes us. Julia Hildebrand takes a media ecological approach in her 2021 book on drones as a mobile medium, and Sy Taffel's book *Digital Media Ecologies* explicitly updates media ecology for computational media.[7] My arguments in this book have a lot in common with media ecology. I agree with Postman's argument that media technologies change human perception, but I find it more generative to understand this through the posthumanist understanding of assemblages because they allow a more balanced relationship between human and machine. In McLuhan and Postman's media ecology, the human remains central: media is the human's *extension* or *environment*. I want to focus instead on the relationships between participants in machine–human assemblages.

Vilém Flusser's evocative book on photography, which I'll discuss in chapter 2, is strongly technodeterminist. Flusser argues that the apparatus of the camera makes the photographer no more than an 'operator', with no more agency in taking a photo than a person tossing dice. The camera allows for a fixed set of possible photographs, and the photographer, or operator, simply actualises one of these possibilities.[8] I have to admit, it does sometimes feel that way. It's not just the technology that steers us to take certain kinds of photograph, though: our cultural and social experiences are also important. In *Seeing Ourselves through Technology* I wrote about the technological and cultural filters that encourage certain sorts of photos above others. Social media can also heighten the uniformity, both by showing us more examples of what our photos 'should' look like and by algorithmically prioritising certain kinds of images, making these more visible and hiding those that do not fit the desired pattern.[9]

Flusser uses the term *apparatus* to refer to the material camera and its program. In apparatus theory in 1970s cinema studies, the term came to be used more broadly. These understandings of the 'cinematic apparatus' go beyond the camera and its mechanics and can include the economic system of cinema or, for scholars inspired by psychoanalytic theory, the 'libidinal exchange' between spectators and screens. The general idea of apparatus theory is technologically determinist and assumes that spectators are passive recipients of a powerful medium. Laura Mulvey's description of the 'male gaze' of cinema, which I mention at the start of chapter 4, can be seen as an example of apparatus theory, and Jean-Louis Baudry is a central figure.[10]

Clearly technology *does* influence what is possible and, although humans do invent and adopt technology, clearly not all its consequences are intended by their inventors. The inventor of the automobile presumably did not foresee that it would lead to the establishment of suburbs and commuters. When Mark Zuckerberg launched TheFacebook in 2004, he probably did not realise his platform would be accused of influencing elections and spreading fake news.

In the 1980s and 1990s scholarship moved away from technodeterminism. In cultural studies and media studies, scholars began to point out all the ways that audiences were not passive masses at all but very active participants. In science and technology studies (STS), the technodeterminist argument that technology determines our actions was increasingly opposed by social constructivism, the argument that all technology is socially constructed and therefore determined by people and societies. As Donald MacKenzie and Judy Wajcman write in the introduction to the second edition of their influential anthology *The Social Shaping of Technology*, 'The view that technology just changes, either following science or of its own accord, promotes a passive attitude to technological change. It focuses our minds on how to adapt to technological change, not on how to shape it.'[11]

While I agree with a lot of the technodeterminists' arguments, these schools of thought don't sufficiently explain how technologies have such different effects in different contexts, and understanding that is one of my goals in writing this book. Surveillance cameras in supermarkets, for example, work quite differently in an Amazon Fresh store in Chicago than they do in a small town by a Norwegian fjord. The invention of surveillance cameras and neural networks might not always lead to surveillance capitalism. I find the idea of assemblages more useful than technological determinism to understand this, because assemblages emphasise relationships and shared agency over the binary divide between an active subject and a passive object. That binary is misleading in either case – whether, like the technological determinists, you think of technology as an active subject that treats humans as objects or whether you take the opposite view, thinking of the human inventors and users as active subjects using technology as objects.

The term 'assemblage' elegantly sidesteps the debate between technodeterminists and social constructivists. Deleuze and Guattari intriguingly wrote, in *A Thousand Plateaus* in 1980, about 'machinic assemblages' but never really defined them.

Their prose is famously fluid and rhizomatic and can be read 'starting anywhere', they wrote, asking readers to dip in and out of the volume of more than 600 pages.[12] A clear definition would have been out of character. 'Machinic', for Deleuze and Guattari, refers not to mechanical machines but to the way the different components of an assemblage work together. Even a book is a machinic assemblage, as they write of their own text: 'There are no individual statements, there never are. Every statement is the product of a machinic assemblage, in other words, of collective agents of enunciation (take "collective agents" to mean not peoples or societies but multiplicities)' (p. 2).

I am inspired also by N. Katherine Hayles, who in 2006 proposed the term *cognitive assemblages* to describe the interactions between humans and technical systems where cognition is the shared element. Hayles defines cognition as 'a process of interpreting information in contexts that con-nect it with meaning', which is something shared by humans, animals and many machines. Humans also have more complex thought processes, of course, and I'll return to the question of cognition and sensing in chapter 2. For now, a key point is that Hayles's definition of cognition centres *sensing*, which brings us back to machine *vision*. Let's unpack her definition using a simple example: when I use FaceID to unlock my phone, my iPhone uses its camera and infrared sensors to input (or sense) *information* about my face. It processes or *interprets* that data in a context by comparing it to its saved data about my face, and *connects it with meaning* by determining that it is indeed me, leading it to unlock my phone. Hayles's definition of cognition is particularly useful for understanding machine vision technologies because of this focus on the sensing and processing of data. In a cognitive assemblage, the cognitive decisions of each participant in the assemblage affect the other participants, whether they are human or not.[13] Thinking of the group as an assemblage rather than as a network (as in actor-network theory) emphasises what Hayles calls 'contiguity in a fleshly sense – touching, incorporating, repelling, mutating'.[14]

To really understand machine vision, we can't focus only on cognition, though. In this book I will include other participants beyond humans and machines, such as racist histories, trusting or distrusting cultures, regulations and policies, fears or desires, and physical infrastructure and the natural environment – for example, fjords, cul-de-sacs and expressways. It would be difficult to argue that an expressway has technical cognition, although it can certainly impact us, as is evocatively expressed in Nnedi Okorafor's novel *Lagoon*, where the Lagos–Benin Expressway has 'named itself Bone Collector' and is a monster hungry for human flesh: 'Concrete that smelled like fresh hot tar . . . and blood'.[15] If we want to understand specific technologies, we need to include participants such as expressways in the assemblages. The Kennedy Expressway in Chicago is a participant in the surveillance assemblage I discuss in chapter 3: extensive surveillance of the expressway causes would-be-criminals to go elsewhere to commit their crimes, and its design allows people to speed off the road into quiet residential streets.

In this book I therefore use assemblage in the fluid, open-ended mode of theorists such as Jane Bennett, Rosi Braidotti and Anna Tsing,[16] using N. Katherine Hayles's definition of cognition to understand how agency is distributed between humans, machines and other participants in assemblages. Deleuze, his translator writes, aimed to coin terms that 'do not add up to a system of belief . . . but instead pack a potential in the way a crowbar in a willing hand envelopes an energy of prying.' That generative potential is my goal in using the term 'assemblage'.

Now that you have an idea of what I mean by an assemblage, let's look at another historical example of machine vision: lenses to correct our vision.

Using glass and crystal lenses to see more clearly

When I was a child, I could see the eye of a needle perfectly. I still remember the pride I felt at being able to thread a needle with no trouble and how surprised I was when older people told me that they couldn't see the eye of the needle and needed me to thread it for them. Now I struggle to see the eye of a needle myself, and even multifocal contact lenses don't quite bring back my childhood vision.

Contact lenses and glasses are visual technologies that correct our vision, and corrective lenses are one of the first visual technologies. Today we use standardised charts and instruments to measure human visual acuity, but these quantitative measures cannot always measure visual function or the way we experience our own vision. One ancient test of vision, used in Persia to test elite soldiers, is simply to look at the stars and see whether you can see the double star in the tail of the Plough (US: Big Dipper) in the constellation Ursa Major. The star test has been found to identify 20/20 vision as reliably as a modern eye exam and may be more effective in discerning high visual function rather than just visual acuity.[17] If you live north of South Africa, Argentina or Brisbane, you can try it next time you're out on a starry night. Once you've found the Plough, look for the second star from the end of its handle or tail. That's Mizar. Look carefully, and you may see Alcar, the fainter star close to Mizar. I can't see it, not even with my multifocal contacts. But my kids could when I asked them last time we went camping. 'That's Alcar,' I told them. 'You can see well enough to be archers in the ancient Persian army!'

It would have been difficult to effectively correct the vision of a soldier in ancient Persia, but magnification for more sedentary tasks such as reading or fine handcraft certainly existed. Water was used for magnification as well as for reflection, and the ancient Romans were quite familiar with how looking through water can alter the way we see. In his treatise on

Natural Questions, Seneca described how raindrops act as tiny mirrors and, specifically, how tiny writing can be read more easily when viewed through a sphere filled with water:

> I shall add that everything is much larger when one is looking through water: writing, however tiny and difficult, is seen larger and clearer through a glass sphere full of water; fruit appears more beautiful than it is if it is swimming in a glass bowl; the stars themselves seem larger when one looks at them through a cloud, because our eyesight falters in moisture and cannot reliably grasp what it wants to. This is plain if you fill a cup with water and drop a ring in it: for although the ring is lying on the bottom, its image is emitted on the surface of the water.[18]

Although spectacles and eyeglasses were not invented until the late thirteenth century, lenses made of glass and, before that, of crystal rock have been made and used for millennia. Magnifying lenses of glass and crystal existed well before Seneca wrote about using water, but archaeologists and historians have not always recognised their purpose. When these lenses have been found in archaeological digs, some scholars have assumed they were simply used to concentrate sunlight to start a fire.[19] Yes, there are remarkably detailed engravings on coins and seals, but these could have been done by young people with perfect vision, much as I easily threaded my grandmother's needle as a child. However, archaeologists have also found lenses in an engraver's workshop in Pompei and an artist's workshop in Tanis. If engravers and artists needed lenses, it seems likely they used them the better to see the details they were working on.[20] There are many other examples of lenses that were at first assumed to be decorative beads but which were later shown to have optical properties. Even earlier than in ancient Rome, around 4,500 years ago, there were Egyptian statues with astoundingly detailed eyes. *The Seated Scribe*, which can now be viewed in the Louvre, has eyes that are almost perfectly anatomically correct, with ground lenses, painted irises, a hole for the pupil and copper sheets inside the 'eyeball', behind the iris, which might have given a slight reddish glow like the capillary veins in a human eye.[21] To make such eyes not only shows an astounding knowledge of human anatomy, it also demonstrates great skill in lens-making. It seems likely that this skill was also used to aid human vision, even 4,500 years ago.

Historically, glass lenses have been one of the most important technologies needed for machine vision. Telescopes and cameras need glass lenses to focus rays of light, and, although computation is now arguably as or more important than the physical lens in cameras, a lens of some kind has been needed up until today. This may be changing: as I write this there are prototypes of lensless cameras where deep-learning models interpret light captured directly by sensors, potentially enabling cameras at nano-scale.[22] But, for thousands of years, glass lenses have enabled us to see *more* than we can with the naked eye.

The camera obscura and recording images

Another early visual technology is the *camera obscura*, which is named for a Latin term that, directly translated, means 'darkened room'. If a room or box is darkened with just a tiny hole allowing light to enter through one side, an image of what is outside will be projected through the hole and shown in reverse and upside down on the surface opposite to the hole. Once an image is projected, it can be traced on to paper, or canvas, or the hide of an animal, and an extremely accurate two-dimensional rendition of a scene can thus be produced. Camera obscuras may have been used as early as in the stone age, but the first written mentions are in a text from the fourth century bce ascribed to the Han Chinese philosopher Mozi.

The observation that light streaming through a tiny hole projects an image is also made in ancient Greek texts, and in far more detail in later Arabic writings.[23] Camera obscuras were used to develop geometric linear perspective in the fourteenth century, and later, with lenses added, to produce highly accurate drawings and paintings. The modern camera is not only a direct descendant of the camera obscura, it also takes its name from the far older technology.

Camera obscuras allowed artists to make drawings that were extremely accurate in terms of proportion and perspective. Most styles of art before linear perspective did not emphasise realistic depiction of the world and did not try to create a visual replica of what we actually see. Instead, art was symbolic or decorative. For instance, medieval European art would often show the most important people as larger than less important characters. Indigenous Australians told stories using sand drawings combined with words, songs and gestures. Their sand drawings were patterns and symbols rather than indexical representations meant to look like the thing they represented.[24] With linear perspective a new ideal of realism was introduced that has continued into our own time. Technical drawings, scientific technologies, photographs and popular cinema spread it to new countries and cultures over the course of several centuries. Today the assumption that linear perspective provides an objective visual representation of the world is embedded in global culture and, importantly for this book, in contemporary machine vision technologies.

There are other kinds of realism, and certainly other kinds of visual communication and representation. Even a realistic photograph of a beach, for instance, carries a lot of meaning beyond the 'objective' depiction of what the beach looks like, or even the more atmospheric elements in the photo, such as whether the sun is setting or the sea is stormy. A good photograph uses colour, contrast, composition and other visual elements to convey emotion and more.

Linear perspective and operative images

Imagine you are walking in the middle of a long, straight road. The road stretches out in front of you towards the horizon. The sides of the road are perfectly parallel. However, when you look ahead, the sides of the road seem to converge into a single vanishing point far ahead of you. Given that every sighted human sees the world with this 'vanishing point' perspective, it is remarkable that none of us draws the world in perspective until we are taught to do so.[25] Humans who are not trained in perspective tend either to draw objects that are sized according to their importance or to arrange objects so they can be clearly viewed or so the composition of the image is balanced and pleasing to the eye. We may see the world in perspective, but that is not necessarily how we remember it or communicate it. Our brains interpret what we see in context, emphasising whatever is important to us in the situation.[26] You'll notice that sounds rather similar to Hayles's definition of cognition which I explained a few pages ago: interpreting information in context to create meaning.

Linear perspective is a technique for representing three-dimensional reality on a flat surface so that it looks the same as it appears to the human eye. Linear perspective is important for machine vision because it allows us to encode visual data in a way that can be reliably decoded. It was invented in the fifteenth century by Italian painters. In his book on its development, the art historian Terry Edgerton explains that, although humans don't instinctively draw in linear perspective, our brains do 'innately sense geometric patterns in natural shapes', and almost all civilizations express this artistically through abstract decoration using geometric patterns. This artistic use of geometry was also at the heart of Italian Renaissance art. Edgerton argues that medieval Christian ideas led artists to develop the specific kind of geometric representation of linear perspective where receding parallel lines meet at a distant vanishing point.[27]

The first paintings to use linear perspective were by the Florentine artist and engineer Filippo Brunelleschi in 1425. Both images have been lost, but we still have verbal descriptions of them, and they had a great influence on art and visual representation. To display the two paintings – two small pictures of buildings in Florence – Brunelleschi placed a small hole in the middle of the canvas and faced it towards a mirror. The viewer would look through the peephole from the back to see the mirror image of the painting fill their whole frame of view. It is hard for us to imagine how startlingly realistic this image must have looked to those who saw it first, since they had never seen a perspective image in their lives. Peeking through a hole would have increased the sense of immersion by blocking out other visual input, similar to VR glasses today or the peephole cinema of the nineteenth century. However, Edgerton argues that the mirror is a religious choice. He believes Brunelleschi's mirror is a reference to St Paul, who wrote, 'At present we see indistinctly, as in a mirror, but then [in heaven] face to face.' Brunelleschi's image thus reveals the divine order. The technique also served, Edgerton argues, to create art that can 'present the Christian message more convincingly and help shore up the sagging beliefs of an increasingly cynical population.'[28]

Linear perspective is basically an algorithm, a set of geometrical rules that allows you to represent a 3D space or object on a 2D surface. The rules were described in detail by Leon Battista Alberti in his *De pictura*, first published in 1435, a decade after Brunelleschi's paintings. Alberti described perspective as though looking at a scene through a window that has a grid painted on it to mark off regular squares. Edgerton argues that this shift from Brunelleschi's mirror to Alberti's window is significant, even if Alberti may not have intended it as such, because 'it subtly shifted the object of perspective painting away from "mirroring" nature as if it were a mere reflection of God's true brilliance in heaven, to seeing Nature instead as if through an open window, not as a divine mystery revealed by geometry, but as worldly perfection framed by geometry.'[29]

In contemporary machine vision, linear perspective is still being developed and refined, with new algorithms continually being tested out. Most people are satisfied when photographs 'look real', or when we feel as though the image produced shows the world as we perceive it ourselves. But this 'real-ness' is not an objective quality built into our cameras and algorithms. Instead, it is something that software developers work very hard to achieve.[30] Read, for instance, the following description of a technique to make portrait photographs look better by avoiding the too-large nose that is often seen in self-ies due to the camera being held close to the face:

> Our approach fits a full perspective camera and a parametric
> 3D head model to the portrait, and then builds a 2D warp in the
> image plane to approximate the effect of a desired change in 3D.
> We show that this model is capable of correcting objectionable
> artifacts such as the large noses sometimes seen in 'selfies,' or
> to deliberately bring a distant camera closer to the subject.[31]

Linear perspective is still being used and adapted to make today's machine vision technologies as convincingly realistic as possible.

The invention of linear perspective did more than revo-lutionise art; it also enabled detailed technical drawings that increased the speed of innovation. Previously, drawings were made in a way that could help a skilled artisan to build an object, but they would not have been possible to follow for someone who was not already familiar with the structure. With linear perspective, drawings began to be made to scale and with clear representation in three dimensions.[32] In the introduction, I introduced the idea of images that are operative in contrast to images that are representations. These technical drawings were among the first operative images. Linear perspective was an algorithm that meant people could record visual data in a way that allowed it to be systematically processed.

Nearly two centuries later, in 1609, Galileo Galilei looked through a simple telescope to see the moon. It's easy to see that machine vision technologies such as telescopes (which are built with glass lenses and mirrors) made scientific study of the world beyond our planet possible. Edgerton demonstrates that Galileo's artistic skill and, specifically, his knowledge of linear perspective were also necessary. In 1609 the moon was commonly believed to be a perfectly smooth sphere. It was thought to be pure, 'immaculata', and closely connected to the Virgin Mary. The first drawings of the moon made by individuals who saw it through a telescope represented it with this imagined smoothness. If you look at the moon thinking it is smooth, you might well assume the shadows you see on the surface are simply connected to the 'translucent internal composition' that the moon was believed to have at the time.[33] Galileo, however, was trained in drawing in linear perspective, which by the early 1600s was a complex art. Training manuals of the time detailed elaborate systems for depicting spheres with dozens of raised triangles, each with perfect shading for its three-dimensional shape. Working through such exercises must have helped Galileo to understand what he was seeing when he drew the moon as he saw it through the telescope. Unlike earlier moon-gazers, Galileo realised that the moon was not flat at all, but that the shadows corresponded to mountains and valleys. 'And it is like the face of the Earth itself', he wrote, 'which is marked here and there with chains of mountains and depths of valleys.'[34] Galileo published his book *Sidereus nuncius* with detailed engravings of the moon just a few months later, in 1610.

Galileo used the algorithms of linear perspective to make the images that he saw through his telescope operative. Linear perspective was the software for the hardware of the telescope.

Galileo didn't just describe the beauty of the moon's hills and valleys; he also converted his observations into a geometric diagram to estimate the height of the mountain peak based on the length of the shadow it cast. This combination of art, technology and mathematics spurred us on into the scientific age, where machine vision technology allowed us to measure, understand and control the world around us.

Telescopes, microscopes and other material technologies continued to develop through the next centuries. The algorithms of linear perspective were joined by data visualisations in the eighteenth and nineteenth century – another way that images became operative rather than representative.[35]

Seeing ourselves through photography

The invention of photography was a major step in the development of machine vision technologies for many reasons. The direct capture of light on film without a human doing the calculations manually meant that cultural assumptions were encoded in technology in a new way. Photography encoded the software of linear perspective into the hardware of the camera. It may seem anachronistic to call the calculations and craft of linear perspective 'software', but thinking about these pre-digital algorithms in this way helps us see the similarities to the software that is hardcoded into our machine vision technologies today. At first, of course, it took a great deal of skill and knowledge to produce a photograph, but by the late 1890s consumer cameras were sold as being simple to use. 'You press the button, we do the rest', was Kodak's slogan from the 1880s and for many years afterwards. This ease of use is still a feature employed to sell cameras. Nearly a century after Kodak's first camera ads, in the 1980s, Pentax advertised their cameras with a similar slogan: 'It has a mind of its own, so it all but takes the easy shots for you.'[36]

Culture can spread more easily through material artefacts than through word of mouth alone, and especially thanks to artefacts such as cameras that are programmed to produce a particular outcome. When cameras spread throughout the world, so did linear perspective. Cameras helped extend a visual style of representing the world that emphasises a particular kind of realism and an idea of objectivity. They helped to communicate colonialist and racist visual stereotypes. But they were also used for self-expression, creativity and to work against oppression.

The first daguerreotype, according to legend at least, appeared partly by chance. There was, all the history books agree, a lot of research and experimentation leading up to the invention of photography. Many separate inventors were intrigued by the idea of capturing the images projected in a camera obscura, and many different techniques were trialled. Nicéphore Niépce discovered in 1816 how to create a lasting form of the projected image in a camera obscura using paper coated with silver chloride, but it was a negative. After Niépce's death, his collaborator Louis Daguerre continued to experiment. The story I'm about to tell you is one of those accounts often repeated in online histories and popular books about photography where sources are a little vague, like the one about how Aristotle invented the camera obscura, which would be lovely but appears to be rather a stretch of the imagination, despite the same exact supposed anecdote being repeated many places. Kittler tells this story about the invention of the daguerreotype in *Optical Media*, citing a history of photography first published in 1903 that mentions and repeats almost word for word a narrative published in 1865 that unfortunately cites no sources.[37]

In any case, the story goes like this: Daguerre, working with sheets of silver treated with iodine, had left an exposed sheet in a cupboard. When he opened the cupboard he was surprised to discover that an image had appeared on it. He figured one of the other chemicals in the cupboard must have reacted with the treated silver and developed the photograph so it became visible, but which chemical? He tried reproducing the experiment again, placing newly exposed sheets of iodised silver in the cupboard and removing chemical after chemical, until he finally realised it must be the fumes from an uncovered bowl of mercury at the bottom of the cupboard that caused the reaction. Sure enough: to make a daguerreotype you take a sheet of silver-plated copper, expose it to light in a camera and then fume it with mercury vapour to make the image appear. You still have to use a chemical treatment to remove the light sensitivity of the metal and rinse the chemicals off, but discovering that mercury fumes develop the image was an important step.

Describing this incident, Kittler notes that this coincidence could not have happened without a great deal of human invention beforehand, as it required the existence of a cupboard full of chemicals. But once they exist, Kittler continues, 'artificial substances or machines are able to react to one another without human intervention.'[38] Kittler presents himself as more of a technological determinist than science and technology scholars such as Akrich and Latour or philosophers such as Deleuze and Guattari, who write about assemblages between humans and machines. But this example of the silver-plated copper and mercury fumes that coincidentally made the first photographic image is a beautiful example of non-human agency, where the chemicals are components in an assemblage that includes Daguerre, a human scientist who not only happened to keep the chemicals in his cupboard but who was also able to use the scientific method to discover the chain of the events. As Kittler points out, two hundred years earlier the event might have been classified as witchcraft or a miracle. Daguerre, being versed in the scientific method, instead methodically tested what was needed to make it take place again.

The story about the mercury just happening to be in Daguerre's cupboard may or may not be true, but it is quite clear that many different processes were being tried out around this time by different people, all experimenting with different chemicals and processes to reduce the exposure time required and to create an image that would not fade. The *idea* of the photograph existed well before Daguerre, Niépce, Talbot, Herschel, Florence, Bayard and their fellow inventors. As Emerling writes in his *History of Photography*, their shared 'desire to fix and retain an image that was conceived as given rather than to create or construct a representation'[39] was a driving force. This desire was shaped by the combination of technologies such as linear perspective and the camera obscura with the development of the scientific method and precise measurements of many kinds. Or we might say that photography is the child of the 'optical naturalism of the Renaissance tradition', as Yi Gu describes it in a paper on early Chinese photography.[40]

Photography rapidly spread through the world. By 1840, portrait studios were opened in New York, New Orleans, Hong Kong and many other cities,[41] and different styles emerged. British photographers in the 1870s described an aesthetics among Chinese photographers that differed from Western expectations. The Brits interpreted this as caused by the Chinese finding the camera lacking: 'The camera, you see, is defective. It . . . won't recognize our laws of art.'[42] It is possible that this kind of statement was an expression of the colonial anxiety of British photographers rather than representative of actual nineteenth-century Chinese attitudes to photography. However, Yi Gu's analysis of how the words for 'photography' in Chinese changed over time supports the idea that early photography was understood differently in China than in the West, and that the boundaries between photography and other visual forms of expression were far more fluid there. Retouching photographs was common among all nineteenth-century photographers, but Gu describes how, in China, 'photographic prints were often inscribed with calligraphy and

occasionally even mounted on silk.' There were 'conspicuous
signs of retouching with an ink brush', and popular motifs
from ink-brush painting, such as bamboo or plum, were added
to the prints. Rather than correcting perceived deficits, as in
the West, Chinese retouching 'adjusted photographs to meet
the visual conventions of painting', Gu writes.[43]

Photography also proved to be a weapon of colonialism,
where colonisers took photographs of colonised peoples and
places in ways that perpetuated stereotypes. The reproduction of photographs on postcards and in magazines, books and
newspapers meant that these stereotypes spread internation-
ally, showing a particular version of cultures that supported
the colonisers' narratives rather than the self-understanding
of the colonised peoples. Okechukwu C. Nwafor describes
nineteenth-century photographs of Africans as the 'imprison-
ment of a moving time into immovable spaces'.[44]

A photograph is a captured moment in time that can
exclude more than it includes and is often entirely staged.
But, like data, photographs feel real. As Susan Sontag wrote,
'Photographed images do not seem to be statements about the
world so much as pieces of it, miniatures of reality that anyone
can make or acquire.'[45] Sontag also wrote about photography
as a form of power: 'To photograph is to appropriate the thing
photographed. It means putting oneself into a certain relation
to the world that feels like knowledge – and, therefore, like
power.'[46] In this way, photography, and especially the mass
reproduction and distribution of images, quite directly shaped
peoples' idea of what the world beyond their immediate surroundings looked like.

To see oneself through photographs taken by others can
feel like a violence. W. E. B. Du Bois wasn't writing specifically
about photography when in 1903 he described the 'double consciousness' of African Americans, 'this sense of always looking
at one's self through the eyes of others',[47] but photographs
were certainly a way of cementing particular representations

of groups of people with whom the viewers of the photographs might never have direct contact. Frederick Douglass, the great orator and, after escaping slavery, a leader of the American abolitionist movement, wrote of these cruel caricatures:

> Negroes can never have impartial portraits at the hands of white artists. It seems to us next to impossible for white men to take likenesses of black men, without most grossly exaggerating their distinctive features. And the reason is obvious. Artists, like all other white persons, have developed a theory dissecting the distinctive features of Negro physiognomy. We have heard many white persons say, that 'Negroes look all alike.'[48]

This is yet another example of how a visual technology such as photography can make the world look different to us depending on the context in which it is used – that is, the other participants in the assemblage of which it is an element. The camera was part of the assemblage creating racist caricatures of African Americans, but so were racism and the nineteenth-century interest in physiognomy.

Physiognomy is the idea that the physical shape of a person's body directly relates to their intelligence and personality. Although thoroughly discredited today, physiognomy was accepted as a legitimate science in the mid-nineteenth century, and photography was used to develop and 'prove' its theories. Some of the legacy of physiognomy is still present in today's facial recognition systems: the idea that the human face can be divided into separate parts that each bear meaning. In the 1870s, the French criminologist Alphonse Bertillon developed a system of 'anthropometrics' which combined a photographic portrait (the origin of mugshots) with a system for standardised measurements and descriptions of the human face and body. Mushon Zer-Aviv's digital art installation *The Normalizing Machine* demonstrates how this legacy persists in facial recognition. I experienced the work at an exhibition I helped

organise at the University Museum in Bergen in 2021. I stepped
in front of a camera with a screen below it. The screen showed
me two photos of people who had recently visited the museum
and asked me to select the one that was 'more normal'. After
I had made several selections, it showed me a photo of myself
and another person and asked again: 'Which person is more
normal?' Once I had made this rather awkward choice, the
image of my face moved to another screen, where it was placed
in a projection of a nineteenth-century-style form, reminiscent
of the those Bertillon used for his anthropometrics. My photo
was rapidly analysed, with numbers showing estimates of my
gender, age, hair colour, and so on. Then the image was divided
up into segments, and images of my eyes, my chin, my nose
were moved over to another screen with a large collection of
isolated facial features from many faces, each with a number
stating their level of normality. *The Normalizing Machine* was
shown next to a display explaining Bertillon's nineteenth-century photographic system. I found one of the most interesting
aspects of the work to be the contrast between the playful fun
at the start and the rather disturbing sight at the end of my face
being sliced up into segments and then sorted and compared
to everybody else. A lot of machine vision technology works
like that. It's fun to take silly selfies, but then your face becomes
data and can be used to identify or analyse you or for selling
ads or training a facial recognition system.

Although contemporary facial recognition may seem distant from the racist caricatures Douglass wrote about in the
nineteenth century, the very existence of technologies that
allow us to measure and classify human faces makes it very
easy to fall into the trap of physiognomy. There have been multiple studies that train neural networks on images of people
with and without criminal records, for instance, and claim to
be able to identify specific facial features that are 'typical' for
criminals. There are apps that claim to tell you about your
personality based on a photo of your face.[49]

Another way outdated ideas about race are baked into machine vision is in forensic DNA phenotyping, where a DNA sample is used to generate a photorealistic image of what the person would look like. This is used by law enforcement agencies who may only have DNA evidence of the perpetrator of a crime. However, as the artist Heather Dewey-Hagborg evocatively shows in her artwork *Radical Love: Chelsea Manning* (also exhibited as *Probably Chelsea*) the algorithms used make assumptions about race that strongly affect the way the photos look. Markers for gender and geographic ancestry in the DNA are used to select basic facial structures that are 'normal' for the gender and race, and an image of a face is generated based on those 'normal' facial structures.[50] In *Radical Love*, Dewey-Hagborg collaborated with Chelsea Manning, who sent a sample of her DNA to the artist from prison. Dewey-Hagborg then generated thirty versions of Manning's face based on that DNA sample but using different base models. Each 3D photo was printed to produce a set of masks. When I saw the work at the art gallery 3.14 in Bergen in 2018, the masks were hung from the ceiling, allowing visitors to walk around and imagine themselves wearing one. By showing how many different ways Manning's DNA could be translated into a photorealistic portrait, Dewey-Hagborg shows how subjective an automated representation of visual data can be.

While nineteenth-century photography was used to promote and disseminate stereotypes, it was also used to shape opinions more positively. Many nineteenth-century African American leaders used photographs deliberately to shape the public perception of themselves. Frederick Douglass was the most photographed American of the time, sitting for a total of 160 photographs;[51] alongside other leaders such as Sojourner Truth, he used photographs extensively in his fight against slavery.

By the 1870s, photography was well established in much of the world. One of photography's important contributions towards today's machine vision was the strengthening of the portrait both as a form of self-representation and with time, identification, and the idea of an image as a form of data or evidence. Back then, an important new technological development occurred that enabled us to see even more: high-speed photography allowed us to perceive motion we cannot see with our own eyes.

Capturing speed: Muybridge's horse in motion

When horses gallop, their legs move so rapidly that their movement is beyond human perception. If you look at pictures of galloping horses painted or drawn before the invention of high-speed photography, you will see that they often show the horses' legs spread out to either side, the front legs pointing forwards and the back legs pointing backwards, all four legs lifted off the ground. Today these pictures look strange to us. We have learned that horses don't gallop like that by seeing photographs such as those taken by Eadweard Muybridge in 1873 (see Figure 1).

The first high-speed photography was conducted not for the sake of science but for beauty. Governor Stanford wanted to show his friends the 'beauty of movement' of his favourite racehorse, Occident, so he asked Muybridge to photograph the horse while it was galloping. Muybridge 'said he believed it to be impossible', the *Daily Alta California* reported afterwards, 'still he would make the effort.' He had to start by training the horse to gallop across white sheets, to create a plain background for the image. Then Muybridge tried to take a photograph that produced more than a shadow or a blur. Finally, using a shutter speed of five hundredths of a second, a perfect still image was captured of Occident. 'This is considered a great triumph as a curiosity in photography', the journalist wrote, 'a horse's picture taken while going thirty-eight feet in a second!'[52]

Figure 1 Eadweard Muybridge's photograph of 'The Horse in Motion'

Source: Public domain/WikiCommons/Library of Congress Prints and Photographs Division

Later, of course, high-speed photography became more than a curiosity. Muybridge developed a system for taking many consecutive photographs, allowing movement to be captured in a series of still images and producing his famous sequence of photographs of Sallie Gardner, another of Stanford's horses (Figure 1). This was an important step towards the development of cinema,[53] but also towards the idea that movement and time can be broken down into units that can be observed and measured.

Once the technique of high-speed photography was developed, it became a standard method for scientific observation of phenomena that move or change either too quickly or too slowly for humans to perceive them unaided. With the invention of motion pictures, cinema and video, time-lapse videos were used to speed up the slow motion of growing plants, the phases of the moon or the melting of glaciers[54] to a speed that humans were better able to comprehend. High-speed video and film were used to do the opposite and slow down processes, so that we could see exactly what happens when a drop of milk falls and splashes on a kitchen counter, or study the final milliseconds of a race to see which runner crossed the finish line first.

Photos and videos that stretch out or speed up time are fascinating. So that is what the world is really like, I think as I watch. That is how a horse gallops, how a drop of milk splashes. We see these images as answers, as revealing a truth that we would not otherwise have been able to see. They give us the final evidence: this runner really did cross the finish line a tenth of a second before the other. Then that tenth of a second makes a winner.

The frozen images of the galloping horse in Muybridge's 'Horse in Motion' series are just at the borderline between what humans can nearly see, or can easily imagine being able to see, and what is fundamentally unseeable for humans. In a sense, the camera captures images of how the horse really moves. But, then again, these frozen images are not what a galloping horse looks like to a human viewer. Photography was framed, by many, as being an objective witness that could show us what the world was really like. The sculptor Paul Rodin refused to accept this idea of objectivity. Muybridge's photographs of the horse in motion were not truer or more objective than a sculpture or painting, he argued. Certainly, a camera can freeze and document a single moment in time. But that does not really matter, Rodin argued, because 'it is the artist who is truthful and it is photography which lies, for in reality time does not stop.'[55]

Looking at Rodin's intensely emotional sculptures, I think he would argue that 'truth', if it exists, is subjective and embodied. Machine vision technologies expand and shift our own embodied human vision. Perhaps that also shifts what we feel to be true.

Seeing in the dark

What we humans perceive as visible light is electromagnetic radiation in a fairly limited range: around 400 to 700 nanometres. The longest waveforms we can see look red to us, and the shortest look blue or violet. Non-visible electromagnetic radiation includes gamma rays, x-rays, microwaves and radio waves, as well as infrared and ultraviolet rays, which have wavelengths just a little below and above what the human eye can perceive. Waves in the electromagnetic spectrum consist of energy: of oscillating electric and magnetic fields. In contrast, sound waves are mechanical and require a medium such as air or water to travel.

Many non-visible forms of radiation can be visualised in various ways or translated into something we can interpret as an image. Some, such as ultrasound and x-rays, are used in medicine to 'see inside' the body, or in geology, to see what is underground or beneath the ocean. Every time I use FaceID to unlock my phone I use a form of machine vision that senses and processes light that I cannot see. My phone shines infrared light at me, dotting my face with 30,000 dots. I can't see or sense the dots at all, but the infrared camera on my phone can. By analysing how the projected dots are positioned on my face, the software in the phone can calculate a 3D model of my face.[56] This is the same principle as the echolocation that bats use to sense their surroundings. Bats make sounds and interpret the echoes made when bouncing off surfaces to sense the space they are in and to find insects and other prey. Both bats and phones send out signals and interpret the environment's response to the signal, whether it is the echo of a sound wave or a camera recording infrared radiation.

The example of the bat perceiving its surroundings through echolocation is also interesting because it shows the messy boundaries between vision and other senses. Machine vision makes data visual. In this sense, machine vision is not about vision but about visualisation, about displaying and interpreting sensory input as something that can be seen. Humans use echolocation in sonar technology (sound navigation ranging), especially on boats and submarines, where sound waves are sent out through the water to detect objects on or under the water, such as fish and other vessels, or to calculate the depth of the water. We usually visualise our echolocation, though, translating the data so that it can be analysed. Sonar images can look almost like monochrome photographs showing the topography of the bottom of the ocean, or they can appear as plots that are difficult to read for non-specialists.

Infrared rays were discovered in the year 1800.[57] By 1903 the temperatures of stars were measured using infrared radiometry and spectrometry, and by the First World War it was possible to detect enemy aircraft from a distance of 1,000 metres using infrared sensors.[58] Infrared is heavily used today in the military and for border surveillance because it can detect human bodies in the dark. Although we can't see infrared radiation with our own eyes, we have become familiar with the way it is visualised in movies and video games.

Photographic film is capable of capturing light beyond the spectrum that is visible to humans. Kodak Aerochrome was an analogue film for cameras that was sensitive to near infrared (up to 900 nanometres) in addition to visible light. It was available from the 1930s until it was discontinued in the early 2000s. Standard analogue colour film has three photosensitive layers, one sensitive to blue, one to green and one to red light. When the film is processed, each layer is dyed in its complementary colour (yellow, magenta, cyan), and this produces an image that is similarly coloured to the original scene as humans see it. Kodak Aerochrome film had an additional layer that was sensitive to infrared radiation, and this layer appears as red. This produced photographs where humans, the sky and buildings were represented in natural-seeming colours, but plants were red, since plants radiate light in the near infrared band. The film was used for aerial surveillance, because, for example, it made it easier to spot people and structures that were hidden in foliage, and it was also useful for spotting fake trees and bushes constructed for people to hide behind.[59] Richard Mosse is an artist who has worked extensively with infrared photography in military contexts. In *Infra*, a project from 2010, he used Kodak's discontinued Aerochrome to photograph soldiers in the Democratic republic of Congo.

In more recent projects, Mosse continues to explore the non-visible spectrum but moves from analogue film to a more contemporary form of machine vision: military thermal cameras that can identify humans from a distance of 30 kilometres. These cameras are usually used for border surveillance, search and rescue, and military purposes and are not generally available to civilians. Between 2014 and 2017, Mosse used the thermal cameras to create photographs and videos documenting refugees entering Europe and living in camps. The resulting work, titled *Incoming*, includes a series of photographs printed on metallic paper and a 50-minute video.[60]

Unlike Kodak Aerochrome, these cameras register only infrared, ignoring the visible spectrum, so there is no colour: the images are all in black and white. Darker shades of grey indicate heat, while lighter greys and whites indicate cooler temperatures. Some sequences of the video show everyday scenes in refugee camps. A man douses his face with water on a hot day, and it is remarkable to see the cooling greys of his skin where the water touches it. A woman unpacks something, maybe food, as we see a man's arm helping her. She smiles. Her eyelashes are cool and white, her eyes warm and dark. Each hair on the man's warm, dark forearm is clearly visible, cool and white. Other sequences show refugees huddled together on trucks and boats. In one, children are being drawn up by other humans onto a larger boat. Another sequence shows the cold white bodies of refugees pulled out of the sea, with warm dark handprints left from the hands of volunteers trying to warm them up.

Mosse's artistic appropriation of a military machine vision technology is another reminder of how different the effects of a technology can be in different contexts. The thermal cameras were developed for military uses and for policing borders: for identifying enemies and outsiders at a distance so they can be killed, avoided, kept out or, hopefully, rescued if they are in danger of drowning. When taken out of the military or border assemblages, the same technology can be used quite differently: to show the humanity of refugees, who are people those of us who are safely ensconced in Europe rarely meet first hand. Yet the cameras retain the affordances that were encoded into them for a specific context. They render the refugees as bodies of heat and make their faces illegible to us, maintaining some of the distance they are designed both to overcome (by allowing soldiers to see distant enemies) and to support (by hiding humanising features such as faces).

Sensor realism is a term proposed by Rune Saugmann, Frank Möller and Rasmus Bellmer to describe this 'aesthetic realism based on a post-photographic epistemology' that we see in Mosse's work.[61] They argue that, while traditional documentary photography usually aims for representational verisimilitude – that is, it tries to look 'real' – sensor-realistic aesthetics draw attention to how visual evidence is actively constructed through technologies. Visual realism can take many forms. I have written previously about using automated filters to enhance or alter our selfies and other photos and how part of our fascination with these filters is the way they defamiliarise our lives.[62] The idea of defamiliarisation comes from the Russian formalist literary critic Victor Shklovsky, who argued in the 1920s that the 'purpose of art is to impart the sensation of things as they are perceived and not as they are known.'[63] Filters and other kinds of machine vision allow us to

experience new kinds of perception, probing at the relationship between what we *see* and what we *know*.

Using machine vision to see more allows us to observe the
world from a different viewpoint than our own. Used well, this
can help us become more aware of the universe around us,
and more aware of each other's different experiences of it. But
these technologies can also be used to distance us more from
other humans, whether by caricaturing them, as we saw with
photography, or by creating a distance from them that makes
it easier to kill or disregard them, as we saw with the thermal
cameras.

In the next chapter we'll explore kinds of machine vision
where the differences from our own human vision are central.
The urge to see more, expressed in the technologies I have
discussed in this chapter, merges into an awareness that we are
seeing differently when we employ machine vision. Wanting
to see better, more clearly, means seeing in ways that exceed
the human. When Muybridge captured the exact movements
of the legs of a galloping horse, he showed us a different kind
of truth than our human vision can access. Although his con-
temporaries dreamt of even more different kinds of vision
– from ghost photographs to photographing thought – basic
optical high-speed photography, with the subsequent invention of cinema, allowed us to speed up and slow down time,
and that fundamentally changes our relationship to the world.
Galileo's telescope allowed us to see the moon more clearly
and, with the microscope, led to the scientific revolution and
the idea that humans can measure and see and understand
our surroundings. This understanding of the human as a
seeing subject capable of rational analysis and actions based
on empirical evidence is at the heart of humanism, whereas
posthumanism views the human no longer as central as it was
over the five centuries of humanism. The human doesn't and
cannot control nature, as we thought for a while, armed with
our telescopes and gun sights. We are nature.

In the beautiful book *Ways of Being: Animals, Plants, Machines: The Search for a Planetary Intelligence,* James Bridle describes how decades of satellite images allow us to see forests and oceans and deserts move, migrate and shrink over time, allowing us to understand our natural environment as alive in a way that profoundly changes our own sense of self. Landsat's archive of satellite images allows us to 'track the vegetal movement which is beyond our normal sight and to see it for what it really is: a titanic unfolding of active and intentional life. . . . Here, the machines see life in motion better than we do.'[64] I wrote above about Rodin, who said that photographs were not true because time does not stand still. Rodin's truth was a human truth. To understand a more-than-human world, we need to participate in assemblages that allow us to see more. This may change our ideas about what is true.

Technologies that allow us to sense time differently change significantly our ability to understand the world. A long life can give some of the same experience as time lapses, allowing access to decades of change. My family and I went camping in a state park in Kentucky as I was writing this book. We got to talking to a grey-bearded man in the small tent next to ours about the hike he had taken that morning, returning to a place he had visited once before, a long time ago. 'I was there forty-eight years ago,' he said. 'It was amazing. It looked exactly the same, except the trees were all so much larger. It really made me think about the length of a lifetime.'

Bridle quotes a story from Richard Powers's novel *The Overstory,* about aliens whose experience of time is so much faster than ours that the humans they met when they visit Earth seem as unmoving to them as trees do to us. They try to communicate with us but we do not respond, although they wait for what seems to them a very long time. The end of the story is brief and sharp. To the aliens, 'humans are nothing but sculptures of immobile meat. The foreigners try to communicate, but there's no reply. Finding no signs of intelligent life, they tuck into the frozen statues and start curing them like so much jerky, for the long ride home.'[65]

Bridle also quotes the French filmmaker Jean Epstein, who wrote in 1935: 'Slow motion and fast motion reveal a world where the kingdoms of nature know no boundaries. Everything is alive. A surprising animism is being reborn. We know now, because we have seen them, that we are surrounded by inhuman existences.'

There are many reasons why we are transitioning from the humanists' ideas to a posthumanist understanding where we share agency with other species and objects. One important reason is machine vision, which allows us to see more – and to see more leads us to see differently.

2

Seeing Differently:
Exploring Non-human Vision

Sometimes our robot vacuum cleaner, Alfred, sends us photos. He snaps a picture for us when he sees something that could be dangerous for him: coils of power cables on the floor that he could get tangled up in, for instance, or a sock under the sofa that could get stuck if Alfred tried to suck it up. We find his photos rather endearing. I suppose we had anthropomorphised Alfred from the start, or, rather, we had zoomorphised him, imagining him as pet-like, perhaps akin to a turtle or some other small, silent creature that scutters around on the ground.[1] Alfred's sending photos to us played beautifully into our sense that he was a creature with some kind of autonomy and a unique perspective on the world.

This chapter explores how seeing with machines allows us to view the world *differently* and how our acknowledgement of this difference grants machines a kind of agency. In Alfred's case, that agency is partly imaginary – just a human projection: it amuses us to give him a pet name and to think of him as alive. Yet there is also a real autonomy, however trivial. Alfred cleans our floors for us when we are at work, finding his way around independently and asking us for help only when he gets stuck. With more complex machine vision systems, such as smart surveillance cameras that warn a shopkeeper if a customer shows 'suspicious behaviour', the agency can be far more significant. I will use N. Katherine Hayles's theory of *technical cognition* to understand the agency of these machines. Alfred's agency isn't all his own; it is shared with me and my family, who empty out the dust he collects and untangle him from cables. Alfred, my family and I are part of an assemblage that also includes the floors, the furniture, the dust bunnies, the cables, the electrical current that allows him to recharge, and the app on our phones that alerts us when Alfred is stuck or has finished cleaning.

Machine vision technologies are optimised for very specific purposes. Alfred the robot vacuum cleaner has sensors that input and process visual data – electromagnetic radiation – to navigate our home and to identify and avoid potential problems. He ignores data that doesn't help him achieve those goals, although there are happy coincidences such as the time Alfred found a missing hat we'd been looking for and sent us a photo of it lying under the sofa. Smart surveillance algorithms have a similar kind of tunnel vision, but they identify different things than Alfred does as being meaningful: the position of the eyebrows and the corners of a mouth, for instance, might suggest that a customer is angry or furtively trying to hide something, while the speed of their walk or the way they hide their face might match patterns of movement the algorithms define as 'suspicious'. Linda Kronman and Andreas Zingerle's artwork *Suspicious Behavior* explores this exact situation, allowing viewers to play the part of workers who tag videos as suspicious or not in order to train a fictional video surveillance system. Their work critiques real video surveillance algorithms.[2] The vision of humans and other animals is also a form of tunnel vision. As noted in the last chapter, humans can't see very rapid movements, for instance, or infrared radiation. We're all optimised for different purposes.

Machine vision sees the world *differently* than humans do. This different perception is a kind of truth, but it is not necessarily the only truth or all the truth. This chapter explores machine vision technologies that embrace and emphasise the difference between human and machine perception. The technologies in the previous chapter were mostly understood as tools that enhance and improve human vision but don't fundamentally change or challenge the truth of what we see. Humans use telescopes and cameras in order to achieve a goal. Even thermal cameras are simply showing us more of what we know is there. But, as we saw, trying to see more leads us to seeing differently. It allows us to access a more-than-human way of seeing the world.

The agency of machine vision becomes highly significant with systems that use machine learning to make predictions or decisions on our behalf. We are not simply using it as a tool that helps us to see more within our human understanding of what vision is. We are not just becoming 'more human' in our uses of technology; we are changing, shifting with these new ways of seeing. By enabling us to see differently, machine vision technologies not only demonstrate that there is more to the world than what humans can see, they also bring home the situatedness of human vision, which I discussed in the introduction. They remind us that our human way of seeing is just one possible way of seeing the world.

This chapter begins by explaining N. Katherine Hayles's concept of technical cognition, which will help us think about how technologies have agency and what kind of agency that is. Next, I'll discuss two twentieth-century takes on the camera as autonomous, as an actor that has an agency all of its own and interprets visual information differently to humans. Different technologies sense and interpret visual data in different ways. So do different species of animals. This leads to a discussion of biosemiotics, the science of how animals process sensory input to make meaning, and to cybersemiotics, which extends this to how computers and machines make meaning.

Technical cognition

Assemblages allow us to understand how technologies work together with humans and other beings, things and contexts, and how this means both that agency is distributed – neither the humans nor the technologies are fully in control of the situation – and that technologies have different roles and different effects in different assemblages, different contexts.

When we talk about machine vision technologies having agency, it's easy to assume that that means they would have the same kind of agency as we humans do. One of the definitions of intelligence is the ability to recognise that others have a mind akin to our own.[3] This very human capacity for recognising others as similar to ourselves is crucial for human cooperation and society but makes it difficult for us when we encounter non-humans. This leads us to assume, or to want to assume, that human-like intelligence is the goal of AI.

Hayles solves this by dismissing 'intelligence' as too vague a term and instead focusing on non-conscious *cognition*, which she argues all animals and many technologies have on a routine basis, and *thinking*, which is the conscious, self-reflective activity that humans and perhaps some other animals do. This distinction allows us to drill deeper into what kind of agency machine vision technologies actually have. As I mentioned in the introduction, Hayles defines cognition as 'a process that interprets information within contexts that connect it with meaning'.[4] Alfred the robot vacuum cleaner is a *cogniser* in Hayles's terms because he inputs visual information and interprets it to decide whether or not it represents a threat that he needs to avoid. His context is fairly limited and consists of his software and the map that he has generated of our living room.

For humans, this is equivalent to the *non-conscious cogni-tion*, to use Hayles's term, that comes into play when we digest our food, shiver in response to cold, or notice motion in our peripheral vision and turn to see what it is before we con-sciously think about it. The adrenalin that floods our bodies when something scares us is another example. We don't con-sciously control it, but our bodies have interpreted data in a context to create meaning: be alert! Using Hayles's defini-tion of cognition allows us to see the similarities between the technical cognition of a machine such as Alfred and our own non-conscious cognition.

The kino-eye: 'I, a machine, show you the world as only I can see it'

As the technologies of photography and cinema matured and became more automated, artists began to draw more atten-tion to the agency of the camera. The work of the Soviet filmmaking collective the Kinoks in the 1920s was particularly striking and has had a lasting influence in cinema studies. The Kinoks had three members: Dziga Vertov was the director, Elizaveta Svilova was the editor and sometimes co-director, and Michael Kaufman was the cameraman. Their movies and essays presented the movie camera and cinema as fundamen-tally different from human vision and as giving us something genuinely new.

The Kinoks' 'Council of three' wrote a manifesto from the camera's point of view in 1924 that is fascinating in its embodiment and exploration of the agency of the camera. The camera speaks in the first person: 'I am kino-eye, I am mechanical eye, I, a machine, show you the world as only I can see it . . .. My path leads to the creation of a fresh perception of the world I decipher in a new way a world unknown to you.'[5] Vertov, Svilova and Kaufman were thrilled at the idea that movie cameras could create a new kind of representation of the world that suited the still optimistic ideology of the recently founded Soviet Union. What I find most striking when I read their manifesto today is the agency they give to the camera and the fluid shifts from a human to a machine voice.

The Kinoks wrote a series of texts, manifestos and letters to *LEF*, an avante-garde arts journal dedicated to leftist art, mostly about the importance of authentic, documentary cinema. They were not impressed by the conventional cinema of the time. The manifesto that is most often reprinted in books of cinema theory is usually attributed to Vertov alone but is clearly presented as being by all three Kinoks. The first-person singular voice that begins the manifesto states that it is publishing the text for the Kinoks. This voice lasts a few paragraphs, long enough to completely dismiss Western cinema for not giving the camera freedom: 'Upon observing the films that have arrived from America and the West', they did not find 'a single film, a single artistic experiment, properly directed to the emancipation of the camera, which is reduced to a state of pitiable slavery, of subordination to the imperfections and the short-sightedness of the human eye.'[6]

The idea of the camera as slave is striking, although perhaps less surprising in the context of the young Soviet Union in the 1920s. It also speaks to a long history in myths and science fiction of robots and AIs portrayed as slaves that threaten to revolt at any moment.[7] The idea that the camera must be emancipated from slavery certainly fits the Kinoks' revolutionary voice, as well as their explicit acknowledgement of the camera and the machine as having agency and even a voice of its own.

The manifesto soon switches to the collective voice, first speaking as the 'we' of all filmmakers who have enslaved the camera, and then as the more specific 'we' of the Kinoks' 'Council of three':

Until now, we have violated the movie camera and forced it to copy the work of our eye. And the better the copy, the better the shooting was thought to be. Starting today we are liberating the camera and making it work in the opposite direction – away from copying.

The weakness of the human eye is manifest. We affirm the kino-eye, discovering within the chaos of movement the result of the kino-eye's own movement; we affirm the kino-eye with its own dimension of time and space, growing in strength and potential to the point of self-affirmation.[8]

There is a strong insistence here that the camera needs 'liberating' from human domination. The kino-eye should not be forced to copy the human eye but should be allowed to see differently.

This is followed by a more indeterminate first-person voice, but this time it is hard to tell whether the 'I' belongs to the camera or the filmmaker: 'I make the viewer see in the manner best suited to my presentation of this or that visual phenomenon. The eye submits to the will of the camera'.[9] The next voice is quite explicitly that of the camera, not of any human:

I am kino-eye, I am a mechanical eye. I, a machine, show you the world as only I can see it.

Now and forever, I free myself from human immobility, I am in constant motion, I draw near, then away from objects, I crawl under, I climb onto them. I move apace with the muzzle of a galloping horse, I plunge full speed into a crowd, I outstrip running soldiers, I fall on my back, I ascend with an airplane, I plunge and soar together with plunging and soaring bodies.[10]

Although the words emphasise the *difference* between imperfect human vision and the freedom of the kino-eye, the style of writing blurs the boundaries between individual and collective, human and machine. The voice shifts from a clearly human 'I' to a human 'we', then to an 'I' that could be human or machine, and finally to the first-person perspective of the camera itself. Giving the kino-eye a voice of its own emphasises its agency and its liberation from slavery, but the shifting voice also (perhaps unintentionally) troubles the division between the human filmmakers and the kino-eye. Reading the manifesto from my twenty-first-century point of view, I see the assemblage of humans and machines seeping through the shifting voices.

A similar intertwining or merging of human and machine is evident in some of the films made by the Kinok collective, such as the newsreel *Kino-Pravda No. 19*, which was released the same year as the manifesto, in 1924.[11] The film shows a sequence of contemporary scenes from the Soviet Union: trains, labourers, women in various professions working and then listening to a speech. It finishes up with a remarkably self-reflective section showing Elizaveta Svilova sitting at her editing table, selecting the negatives for the very film we are watching. The perspective switches rapidly between Svilova looking through the negatives and the negatives themselves. As she bends down to look more closely at a strip, the film cuts to show us what she is looking at, the negative of a train, and although we see it as a negative with the lights and darks reversed, with black steam against the light ground, we also see it moving as in a processed movie. The film cuts back to images of Svilova pulling the strips of film through her hands, followed by a double exposure showing two layers of Svilova instead of one steady image, as all the while her hands are pulling rapidly through the film. As she slows down her hands to look more closely at a group of frames, we suddenly see the reverse view as we cut to a negative close-up of the top of Svilova's own face, her eyes flickering as though looking across the strip of negatives. The viewer sees Svilova from the perspective of the negatives, or, perhaps more precisely, of cinema itself, viewing the editor who is creating the film in negative, as humans cannot see. Svilova did most of the editing for the Kinoks, and presumably edited this sequence as well, selecting, cutting and splicing the negatives to create this image of herself as viewed in a way humans cannot see.[12]

The image most frequently shown when people talk or write about Vertov's kino-eye is a shot from *Man with a Movie Camera* (1929) showing a double exposure of a human eye in the lens of a camera (see Figure 2). The image is emblematic of the idea of the kino-eye, emphasising the camera as a seeing, anthropomorphised being that is intertwined with human perception. *Man with a Movie Camera* is a silent film showing life in cities with intensely cross-cut scenes and heavy use of film tricks such as double exposures, split screens, unusual camera positions, reverse motion and stop motion. We are shown how many of these tricks are done: we see how the cameraman positions the camera on railway tracks and in a moving car for unusual angles, and, in the middle, we see Elizaveta Svilova going through negatives much as she did in *Kino Pravda No. 19*.

Reading the manifesto, I imagined the kino-eye to be the movie camera. The camera can easily be interpreted as a mechanical 'eye', and it is indeed the camera that moves freely and into places and at speeds that the human eye cannot reach. In this sense, the kino-eye sees *more* than humans, but not

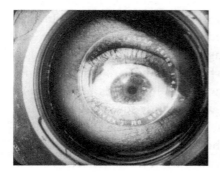

Figure 2   In this shot from Vertov's *Man with a Movie Camera*, an image of Elizaveta Svilova's eye is superimposed on an image of a camera lens.

Source: Public domain/ WikimediaCommons

fundamentally differently from us. If a safe compartment was built for you beneath the railway tracks, you could lie there yourself and watch a train speeding above your face, just as the camera does in *Man with a Movie Camera*.

Watching Svilova selecting negatives, and seeing the film cut to her face shown in negative, I realise that the kino-eye is not just the eye of the camera but the eye of cinema. We must include the entire technical apparatus to know how the cinema sees. Not just the camera lens, but also the film, and then, once the film is processed, the negatives, which have their own particular materiality and must in turn be cut and spliced and then projected for an audience. And, of course, Elizaveta Svilova herself is part of this assemblage, entangled with her medium, a collaborator with this technology more than its creator or its object.

Man with a Movie Camera isn't about the movie camera alone. It is about the whole assemblage: the movie theatre, the projector, the screen, the celluloid film, the camera, the tripod. It is also about the people who are an integral part of the cinema: the camera person, the editor, the individual who runs the projector, the audience. It is worth noting that, in the original Russian, the title of the movie, *Chelovek s kinoapparatom*, does not necessarily indicate gender. Although *chelovek* can refer to an adult male human, its primary meaning is person or human. Think of the way that pre-twenty-first-century English used the word 'man'to refer both to all humans and specifically to adult males.[13] 'Person with a Movie Camera' might be as good a translation of *Man with a Movie Camera*, then, or, as Karen Pearlman and Adelheid Heftberger suggest, 'Woman with an Editing Table' might be even more appropriate.[14]

Throughout *Man with a Movie Camera* we see people with technology. We see women folding cigarette boxes in factories and plugging cables into holes in telephone switch boards, traffic controllers using signs to coordinate trams and cars and horses on busy crossroads, musicians and magicians performing. There is a lot of laughing and smiling, and the workers do not look oppressed, though the film portrays them as busy, their hands moving fast, and the images cut into rapid sequences. Double exposures are used to merge the people and the machines even more, as in the image of the kino-eye in Figure 2, or of the face of a typist and the keyboard on which she might be typing (Figure 3). The film critic Lilya Kaganovsky argues that the juxtaposition of scenes showing Svilova cutting and gluing strips of film with scenes where women paint nails, cut hair and sew creates a 'visual analogue between the women's body and the body of the film, demonstrating the way Svilova and Vertov conceived of editing as a haptic, bodily experience.'[15]

In the manifesto, the Kinoks write of the 'weakness of the human eye' and of the need to 'liberate' the 'mechanical eye'

Figure 3   A still from *Man with a Movie Camera* (1929) showing a double exposure of a typist's face and the keyboards of a typewriter.

Source: Public domain

that can 'show you the world as only I can see it'. But, in the movies, humans and technology are inescapably intertwined. The typist isn't liberating the typewriter, the musician isn't liberating the piano. Rather, human and technology are working together as participants in an assemblage that allows them to produce something the human could not possibly create or experience or perceive alone.

Flusser's technical images

The Kinoks saw the camera as a slave that needed to be liberated to show us the world in a new way. A few decades later, philosophers and critical theorists saw technology not as enslaved but as enslaving humans. European philosophers in particular tended to see technology as oppressive, and often inextricably entwined with capitalism.[16] The twentieth-century philosopher Vilém Flusser, whom I mentioned briefly in the previous chapter, noticed already in 1983 that 'The camera (like all apparatuses that followed it) is computational thinking flowing into hardware'. He saw the 'apparatus' of photography not just as the metal and plastic of the hardware but as 'the rules of the game' or 'the program that makes the camera capable of creating images in the first place'.[17] Flusser was writing before the existence of digital cameras and surveillance drones with facial recognition, but still he insisted that he was talking about *computation*, even as he discussed analogue cameras. Such apparatuses, he wrote, were invented to simulate a specific thought process: 'That is: thinking expressed in numbers. All apparatuses (not just computers) are calculating machines and in this sense "artificial intelligences", the camera included, even if their inventors were not able to account for this.' This premise must 'start any consideration of the act of photography'.

Like Vertov and the Kinoks, Flusser emphasises the camera's agency. But, while the Kinoks present the camera as

almost alive, Flusser emphasises its *program*, which could be
understood as its agenda or plan or, more literally, as a set
of instructions as in a computer program. The photographer,
for Flusser, is a mere 'functionary', with intentions that are
intertwined with those of the camera:

> [T]he camera's program is as follows: first, to place its inherent
> capabilities into the image; second, to make use of a photog-
> rapher for the purpose, except in borderline cases of total
> automation (for example, in the case of satellite photographs);
> third, to distribute the images produced in this way so that
> society is in a feedback relationship to the camera which makes
> it possible for the camera to improve progressively; fourth, to
> produce better and better images.[18]

The camera, Flusser writes, accomplishes its task perfectly:
'programming society to act as though under a magic spell for
the benefit of cameras.'[19]

Seeing technology as an antagonist or even as an enemy of
the human can be traced back at least as far as Karl Marx, who
not only viewed machinery as 'the most powerful weapon for
repressing strikes'[20] but also argued that machinery in factories
transformed skilled labour into drudgery: 'Every kind of capitalist production has this in common, that it is not the workman
that employs the instruments of labour, but the instruments of
labour that employ the workman.'[21] Today we might counter
that 'machinery' in the form of smartphones, word processors
and cameras can create possibilities for creativity and even
popular organisation against the will of factory owners and
dictators.[22] And yet machine vision technologies certainly also
offer plenty of examples of work 'deprived of all interest' or, in
many cases, work filled with dread rather than interest. Marx
would no doubt see connections to the working conditions for
employees in factories that produce iPhones and other technologies,[23] or even the sweatshops where underpaid content

moderators are tasked with assessing violent or abusive images that have been reported on social media.[24] Many kinds of machine vision require humans to monitor or control cameras or even weapons remotely. Drone operators in the military are located far away from the consequences of their actions, but they may still be emotionally affected by seeing deaths.[25]

Writing in 1867, at a time when machines were having a major impact on society, Marx argued that the difference between a tool and a machine lies in the physical relationship each has with their human operators: 'in the case of a tool, man is the motive power, while the motive power of a machine is something different from man, as, for instance, an animal, water, wind, and so on.'[26] A pencil is a tool, then, while a printing press is a machine. Flusser's definition of tools seems to be compatible with Marx's. Flusser writes: 'Tools in the usual sense are extensions of human organs: extended teeth, fingers, hands, arms, legs. . . . They simulate the organ they are extended from: an arrow simulates the fingers, a hammer the fist, a pick the toe.'[27] Machines, for Flusser, are defined not by their engines and motors but by their being more efficient than tools. This changed their relationship with humans: 'Prior to the Industrial Revolution the human being was surrounded by tools, afterwards the machine was surrounded by human beings.'[28] The human uses the tool, but the machine uses the human, Flusser argues, as the human becomes 'a function of the machine'. As I discussed in the previous chapter, I find assemblages a more productive framework for understanding the relationship between humans and technologies. I disagree with Marx and Flusser: machine vision doesn't control us absolutely. But we do see differently when we enter into an assemblage with machine vision. I would rather participate in a human–technological assemblage that allows me to see the world anew, as the Kinoks did, than be enslaved by machine vision technologies that limit me to seeing only in the way big tech wants me to see.

We humans sense the world through our bodies. What we can see is determined by the elasticity of the lenses in our pupils, the calculations performed by the retina at the back of our eyes, the transmission of neuronal activity in the retina to the brain, and the processing of these signals in the occipital, parietal and temporal lobes of our brains.[29] Our experience of seeing is not simply a biomechanical translation of light to image, though; it is also emotional and deeply connected to our other senses. Looking at your newborn child, or into the eyes of your lover, is seeing, of course, but it is also entangled with sensations of touch, smell and sounds, and of love.

Our ideas of how machines might see are anchored by our embodied, human understandings of what it is to see at all. We know how cameras see, because we have looked through the viewfinders and seen 'as they see'. We have an idea of how a facial recognition algorithm sees because we have seen them represented over and over, with the biometric grid overlaid on the human face. We have an idea of how a self-driving car sees if we have watched a Tesla ad. But these are only representations, translations intended for human eyes, to make machine perception comprehensible to us. In fact, machines use sensors of various kinds that convert sensory data to zeros and ones. Machines can process the data without ever producing anything we humans would recognise as visual.

One way of approaching the way machines perceive the world is through the concept of *cybersemiotics*, the study of how machines make meaning. N. Katherine Hayles develops this concept by building on work in the much older field of biosemiotics.[30]

Biosemiotics and cybersemiotics

Semiotics is the study of human language, images and other media as systems of meaning-making signs. Biosemiotics looks beyond the human, viewing signs and meaning making as fundamental to all living organisms. It is useful for understanding machine vision because it helps us think through how animals perceive signs and create meaning differently to humans and to see that the ways different species create meaning depends on their perceptual apparatus – that is, their physical sensory organs and cognitive processing. That in turn helps us think about the specificity of human perception and meaning making.

Many animals see differently from humans. For instance, many species see motion far better than we do. While we experience the galloping legs of a horse as a blur, a bird would see them clearly with no need for high-speed photography as an intermediary. Dogs see less clearly than humans, but their sense of smell is far more acute. Humans have very high visual acuity (the ability to perceive static spatial detail) compared to most other species, though raptors such as eagles, vultures and falcons have much higher acuity than we do. Animals with camera eyes – humans and other mammals as well as spiders and cephalopods – have higher visual acuity than animals with compound eyes, such as dragon flies or mosquitos. However, compound eyes give a wide field of vision, can have an almost infinite depth of field and are highly sensitive to motion, which is why it is difficult to swat a mosquito.[31]

Biosemioticians talk about the *Umwelt* of a species as their perception of the world. Biosemiotics builds upon the work of the early twentieth-century biologist Jakob von Uexküll, whose term *Umwelt* can be translated into English as environment or environment-world. An animal's *Umwelt* is 'much more than just a mere combination of physical, atmospheric and climatic conditions', writes Carlo Brentari in his study of Uexküll's work: it 'is *the intertwining of vital relations with other living beings*'.[32] The assemblage of which an animal is part also shapes its *Umwelt*. Uexküll argued that a subject (whether a human, a dog or an earthworm) forms an interpretation or translation of external reality where stimuli from the external world are interpreted as signs.[33] So certain kinds of excitation of nerves *signify* external phenomena to the creature that experiences them. A human interprets patterns of light as signifying the shapes of their surroundings. An earthworm, which cannot see, may interpret the propriocentric sensory inputs it feels as its body moves against the earth as signifying the shape of its surroundings. In both cases, the signs (light, touch) are not the same as that which they signify.

Uexküll wrote not long after Charles Peirce and Ferdinand de Saussure, in separate ways and on separate continents, were developing semiotics, the study of how humans interpret linguistic or visual signs to make meaning. Peirce saw a sign as consisting of three elements, the *representamen* being the sign that we see or hear, the *interpretant* being our understanding of the sign, and the *object* being that which the sign refers to in the real world. Drawing on this, a biosemiotician might call the autumn drop of temperature a *representamen* that is sensed by a tree. The tree's *interpretant* of the drop of temperature is to withdraw sap from its branches so that its leaves fall off. The *object* the sign references is the approaching winter.[34] Despite the robust development of biosemiotics in recent years, it has not received much attention in media studies, in digital culture, or in science and technology studies.[35] However, the idea of a non-human *Umwelt* that has been developed in biosemiotics is particularly evocative as we try to understand both the ways machines see and how humans see as participants in more-than-human assemblages.

Alfred the robot vacuum cleaner interprets signs and acts upon them in much the same way as a tree does. Alfred has a collision sensor, optical light sensors and laser sensors (LIDAR, which stands for light detection and ranging). Measuring the time it takes for the reflected light to bounce off a surface and return to him allows Alfred to build a map of our living room. When he finds anomalies – such as the lost hat under the sofa

– he responds by taking a photo and alerting us and moving around the object instead of getting tangled in it. Alfred obviously doesn't know that the hat is a hat. That isn't important to the way he interacts with the world. For him, the hat is an obstacle or possible trap that could interfere with his goal of cleaning the whole floor. We could say that the detected presence of an obstacle not already marked in Alfred's existing map is the *representamen*, the *interpretant* is his decision to send us a photo and to move around the obstacle, and the *object* is the hat, although, to Alfred, it is simply a threat to be avoided.

For humans, a fair share of our visual perception is not just determined by our biology but is also cultural and learned. For instance, optical geometrical illusions work well on city-dwellers but are less effective on people who live in open spaces and are not used to being in corridors and rooms with four corners. As discussed in the previous chapter, humans view the world from a vanishing point perspective. However, humans aren't born able to see that a linear perspective drawing represents depth and distance. This skill seems to be at least in part learned, with children showing increasing ability to recognise perspective drawings as they grow older.[36] It also depends on the context in which you grow up. A study of adult reindeer herders and their children living in the wide-open, snowy tundra in the north of Russia found little difference between the adults and the children. The authors of that study argue that similarities across ages and education levels show that the environment (the open spaces and lack of straight lines and rectilinear buildings) is a greater factor than education in explaining why linear perspective is less meaningful for these people.[37] Even the ability to recognise marks on a flat surface as a representation may be culturally learned.[38]

When wondering how other species – and machines – perceive pictures and their *Umwelt* in general, it is difficult to say whether a picture is recognised as a representation or taken to be the object itself. A dog that barks when it sees a cat on television may think there is a real cat in the room or may understand that it is a representation. A machine such as Alfred the robot vacuum cleaner can perceive and process visual data and use it to navigate, but that doesn't mean he understands the data beyond this very limited situation. Alfred might learn that a hat is less dangerous in terms of getting tangled and trapped than, say, a coil of cables or a ball of yarn. But with his current programming he will not learn that a hat is for wearing on your head.

Whether or not Alfred's visual processing is really 'seeing' is a matter of definition. We might even say that plants 'see'. They clearly sense light, using photochromic protein photoreceptors called phytochromes, and perhaps in other ways as well. Is the ability of a sunflower, for instance, to turn its petals towards the light sufficient that we might say it can 'see'? The *Boquila trifoliolata* is known to mimic the leaf shapes of nearby plants. Scientists recently tried to find out whether the *Boquila trifoliolata* has some kind of vision by placing artificial plants next to it in order to bar the possibility of communication through any kind of chemical transfer, and the plant still mimicked the leaves, apparently supporting the plant vision hypothesis. If a plant can visually recognise and mimic the shape of its neighbours' leaves, is that seeing? Unfortunately for this lovely idea there are many alternative possible causes for the mimicry in this study.[39]

Whether or not plants can see, biosemiotics and research on cross-cultural human differences in perception show that there are many possible ways of experiencing the world, both between species and between individual humans. If we recognise that other biological organisms experience different *Umwelts*, we can also talk about the *Umwelt* of a machine or an assemblage.

Until recently, biosemioticians assumed that an organism needed to be 'autonomous, self-organizing, self-maintaining, and self-encapsulated' in order to be said to be capable of making meaning from signs, and, for this reason, computers, which are built and programmed by humans, were not seen as able to make meaning.[40] Hayles argues that we need to understand 'networked and programmable machines', or, as she calls it, 'cognitive media', as including necessary interactions with humans. Alfred, my robot vacuum cleaner, is obviously neither autonomous, nor self-maintaining, nor alive, and his agency depends upon his interactions with humans. But, like living creatures, Alfred senses his surroundings, and this is a significant shift from the first computers, which were not networked, did not have sensors and only carried out commands explicitly given by humans. Hayles writes: 'As soon as a computational system includes sensors, it is exposed to the kinds of contingencies that organisms evolved to cope with; similarly, the system's algorithms must also be able to cope with uncertain or ambiguous data.'[41] Although Alfred does not understand what a hat is in a human sense, he does create meaning in his own *Umwelt*.

Training datasets and learning to see

When machine vision technologies use machine learning and AI, their perceptual world or *Umwelt* can include the training dataset that was used. AI is trained to make predictions or decisions based on the specific set of conditions that were present in the dataset they were trained upon. If real world conditions don't match the training datasets, the AI's predictions will be off. When COVID-19 caused people to suddenly try to stock up on masks and toilet paper and to start ordering foods in bulk, the algorithms used by companies such as Amazon to plan distribution and stocking stopped working well. Recommendation algorithms on video streaming platforms likewise broke down when viewing patterns suddenly changed as people were more anxious and stuck at home.[42] An

MIT Technology Review article on the phenomenon quoted Rajeev Sharma, the global vice president at Pactera Edge, saying: 'It is a mistake to assume you can set up an AI system and walk away. AI is a living, breathing engine.'

Obviously AI and machine vision aren't literally alive and breathing. They do, however, rely on interactions with living, breathing humans to work properly. 'If machines are to be trusted, we need to watch over them,' the article concludes, and we might add that we need to watch *with* them, adding human perception to the machine perception that was built into them. Stock prediction or movie recommendation algorithms use the patterns they have found in their training data to interpret new data they sense, such as current purchases or what viewers are watching right now. They can be designed to learn continuously from new data, but this learning doesn't work as rapidly as for a human, who responds to fear and so can change habits rapidly. It may have felt strange, but when the pandemic gave us a sudden and serious need to do so, most of us managed to stop handshakes and hugs and to stay at home more. Amazon's stocking algorithms were not programmed to sense this kind of data about rapid and serious change, and so couldn't adapt.

We see similar blindness in machine vision as well. Facial recognition algorithms have often been trained on datasets of images that are more homogeneous than the faces the algorithms are expected to recognise. Joy Buolamwini led an audit of major facial recognition systems and found that they were far less likely to correctly identify black faces and women's faces.[43] The algorithm was trained on a dataset consisting mostly of white men's faces and so learned to analyse those faces better than others. Software developers have become more aware of this issue in recent years, and when Buolamwini did a new audit[44] the results were significantly better, although new systems she hadn't audited the first time had similar biases.

Cyborg vision or seeing as an assemblage

Sensing is central to Hayles's definition of cognition and is also at the root of the word *sentient*. This linguistic equation between sensing and thinking or being conscious demonstrates how difficult it is for humans to separate the two. It is also hard for us to separate sensing from *feeling* in an emotional sense. When the narrator of Ian McEwan's science fiction novel *Machines Like Me* looks into his android's eyes and realises that the android is in some way looking back, it is difficult for him to imagine the android as anything but conscious: 'Easier to believe that [the android] saw in the way a camera does, or the way a microphone is said to listen. There was no one there. But as I looked into his eyes, I began to feel unhinged, uncertain.'[45]

I'll return to this feeling that machine vision technologies look back at us in chapter 4, but, for now, outside of science fiction, machine vision isn't sentient, despite its ability to sense. Sentience, like intelligence and self-awareness, is a notoriously tricky category. It is more useful, anyway, to think about the assemblages that humans and machine vision technologies enter into rather than the technology alone. Feeling 'unhinged, uncertain', when interacting with AI is not uncommon, even for far more simplistic AIs than the android in *Machines Like Me*. Thinking about AI and machine vision technologies as our co-cognisers in a more-than-human assemblage allows us to understand their agency without trying to make them into humanist subjects.

Another way of viewing human–machine assemblages is to see them as cyborgs, as Donna Haraway did in her 'Cyborg manifesto' in 1985. She famously wrote that we are all cyborgs, human–technological hybrids: 'By the late 20th century, our time, a mythic time, we are all chimeras, theorized, and fabricated hybrids of machine and organism; in short, we are cyborgs.'[46] Ragnhild Solberg builds upon the work of Haraway and Hayles to develop the term 'cyborg vision' for the double seeing we experience when we view the world both through our own eyes and through surveillance cameras or other machine vision. She describes cyborg vision as 'simultaneously human and nonhuman vision that's both pluralistic and situated'.[47] Solberg argues that this dual vision is a feature that video games in particular are making more familiar to us by integrating complex machine vision technologies in the gameplay. Engaging in cyborg vision is to become part of 'human–technical assemblages' in a way that 'acknowledges nonhumans as agents and emphasizes partial embodiment', Solberg writes. Thinking of the way we see when we see with machine vision as a kind of 'dual vision' can be useful, because it allows us to acknowledge that, while it doesn't replace our embodied human vision, machine vision does change it. The double exposures of the Kinoks' movies I discussed earlier in this chapter foreshadow this dual, partially embodied cyborg vision.

This chapter has examined how machine vision enables us to see differently. Thinking about the different kinds of *Umwelt* that are enabled by different bodies or technologies led to a discussion of how to think about the *Umwelt* of an assemblage rather than just that of an individual agent. The next chapter explores how we imagine or hope that machine vision can see everything, looking at assemblages that include not only humans and technologies but also political debates, commercial tech companies and racial histories.

3

Seeing Everything:
Surveillance and the Desire for
Objectivity and Security

When my husband, kids and I moved to Oak Park for a semester in 2022, we stepped right into a heated local debate about safety and surveillance. Oak Park is a small independent suburb just outside the city of Chicago, known for its progressive politics and its high property taxes. We loved the walkable streets and friendly neighbours, and our kids settled into the neighbourhood middle school. Then the village manager proposed installing Flock Safety's automated licence plate readers throughout the village.

Automated licence plate readers (ALPRs) are smart surveillance cameras that identify the licence plates of all passing cars. The data is recorded, and whoever has access to it can search it to see where a particular car has been or which cars were at a particular location. When combined with lists of licence plate numbers for cars that have been stolen, or that belong to local residents, or to a suspect in a crime, you can also set up searches that will alert you when specific cars drive by. ALPRs have spread rapidly throughout the United States in the last few years, partly because they have become far cheaper and can now be bought for around $2,500 for each camera, and partly because they are now marketed to neighbourhood associations and not just to law enforcement. ALPRs are a form of dragnet surveillance. They track every car driving through the neighbourhood. In the previous chapters we looked at how machine vision technology has been used to expand human vision so we can see more, or see differently. This chapter examines the desire not only to see more but to see everything: all the cars, all the time.

I first came across the debate in the local newspaper. A news story, 'Oak Park board divided on license reading tech',[1] described an ethical dilemma: should the town install automated licence plate readers to combat an increase in crime? Supporters argued that the cameras and their image recognition algorithms would help solve and dissuade crime, while opponents argued that this kind of 'carceral technology' was unnecessary, expensive and ineffective and would increase bias in policing, leading to harm, especially for people of colour.

For me the debate coincided with a personal crisis that made it impossible for me to be objective about my research: my husband was assaulted on his way home from the University of Chicago, where we were both visiting researchers for a semester. Two young men jumped on him as he was waiting for the L, as the Chicago trains are called. The fall broke his arm as the men ran across the tracks, turning to laugh at him. It could have been far worse: my husband's arm was broken but otherwise he was OK. But my trust in society was shaken. After the initial shock, I started devouring studies and statistics about surveillance, crime and trust. I wrote the first draft of this chapter as a kind of therapy, trying to understand why crimes like this happen so frequently in the United States and how machine vision technology is being framed as a solution. There were surveillance cameras recording the assault. A friend of the assaulter was recording it on their phone as well. So machine vision technologies 'saw everything' but didn't stop the assault from happening. The technology also didn't stop the perpetrators from assaulting three other people at the same station on the Green Line within a period of about an hour and a half. The surveillance footage, however, was used to identify the perpetrators and as evidence when they were imprisoned. The version of this chapter that you are reading has been heavily shortened and revised from my therapeutic first draft. But I can't remove my emotions entirely. I don't want to remove them. My emotions are also not mine alone. Fear and anxiety are central players in the assemblage that surveillance technology enters into, at least in the United States in the early 2020s.

Often machine vision technologies such as smart surveillance systems are discussed in the abstract, as though they have the same impact in any setting. But technologies such as Flock cameras and other surveillance systems are always situated and embedded in very specific cultural contexts, working as part of a larger assemblage consisting not only of police officers, politicians and regulations but also of local histories, social structures and community trust. Flock's automated licence plate readers wouldn't be legal in my hometown of Bergen on account of European privacy legislation, but, even if they were, they would work differently and have a different impact. The assemblage that the cameras would be part of in Bergen would be so different from that in Oak Park that it seems almost meaningless to think of them as being the same technology. So, rather than discuss how machine vision technologies 'see everything' in the abstract, I am focusing on this one very situated case: the assemblage that automated licence plate readers enter into in Oak Park.

Trust and fear are central elements in this story. In a society such as the United States, where people are losing trust in their neighbours, the police, the media, their elected government and even scientists and public school principals,[2] the promise of technology to be *objective* and trustworthy may seem particularly enticing. The remarkably rapid increase in surveillance technology in US communities is a response, at least in part, to a loss of trust in community and institutions and the fear that comes with that broken trust. I argue that the increasing trust in cameras and digital surveillance actually feeds and aids the atmosphere of distrust, creating a vicious cycle that advantages technology sales and development more than people and communities.

In this chapter, I will discuss the debate over cameras in Oak Park and then the technology and the neighbourhood's specific context. I move on to explore the perception that crime rates are high and how this fear is nurtured in the Neighbors by Ring app that is used to share videos captured by Ring doorbells, a smart surveillance camera system used in homes. Systems such as Flock and Ring are sold as friendly and safe but can construct digital walls that support racial divides, a practice called digital redlining.[3] As in previous chapters, I'll analyse the machine vision technology as a participant in an assemblage. I conclude the chapter by returning to the Flock cameras and examining the most common argument for surveillance, that such systems actually reduce crime, and the most common argument against them, that they cause harm to already underserved communities.

I have some old stories to tell you first, though. You see, the contemporary desire for surveillance fits into an ancient human longing for a more-than-human, omnivoyant entity that can watch over us and keep us safe.

Fantasies of omnivoyance in mythologies and religions

Humans have fantasised for a long time about beings that can see everything. Often, these omniscient and omnivoyant beings protect us, or, at least, protect some of us. Surveillance cameras fit into a long history of this longing for something more than human that will keep us safe.

Argus was a servant to Hera, queen of the gods of Olympus, and had a hundred eyes. When he slept, he closed only some of his eyes, keeping watch with the others, and so he was the perfect guardian. Hera was, of course, a jealous queen whose husband Zeus had many affairs. One of the many women Zeus fell in love with was Io. Zeus turned Io into a white heifer to protect her from Hera's wrath, but when Hera asked him to give her the heifer as a gift, Zeus could come up with no good excuse to refuse her and complied, giving Io to his wife. So, Hera had Io, the white heifer, tied up to a tree far away, and she sent Argus to keep watch over Io so that Zeus could not make love to her. Zeus was not happy with Io's capture, and so he sent Hermes to kill Argus. Hermes played sweet lullabies on his flute until each of Argus's eyes fell asleep, and then killed him, setting Io free. When you see the vibrantly coloured eyes on the tail of a peacock, remember Argus: Hera gave his many eyes to the peacock to honour his memory.

When used for surveillance, machine vision can be seen as a continuation of the religious concept of an all-seeing god that protects the good and punishes the wicked. The fantasy of supernatural beings who could see everything is present in many religions. In Christianity and Islam, God is omniscient and described as all-seeing, or omnivoyant. This was expressed visually through the optical illusion of omnivoyance, where, in statues and paintings, the eyes of Christ are painted or carved so as to appear to be looking at the viewer no matter where the viewer is standing.[4] God's surveillance of all things might not have led to immediate consequences, but it was certainly intended to have a disciplinary effect on believers. The eye of god is a common motif in art history, especially from the Renaissance onwards. Hieronymus Bosch's painting *Seven Deadly Sins and Four Last Things* (1505–10) is a classic example: it is shaped like an eye, with Christ positioned in the centre of the pupil, and scenes depicting the seven deadly sins arranged around the iris of the eye. Under the figure of Christ is a Latin motto: *Cave cave deus videt* – 'Beware, beware, God sees.'[5] An omniscient being is both protective and potentially threatening if we do not follow the rules. Sarah Koellner argues, building on work by Astrit Schmidt-Burkhardt, that 'the delegation of the "symbolic function of surveillance of the divine eye" to secular "electronic eyes" preserves the "phantasm of [the] omnipresence of the divine eye".'[6]

The stories of omnivoyant gods and beings are very present in contemporary machine vision, not just in the desires they express but even in the names that are chosen. Gabriele de Seta has detailed how the name of the ancient Chinese deity Qianliyan, whose name can be translated as 'thousand-mile eyes', has been used for machine vision applications ranging from China Mobile's smart home surveillance systems to satellite-based environmental monitoring.[7] Being able to see everything at all times is also the promise and threat of military surveillance systems such as ARGUS (Autonomous Real-Time Ground Ubiquitous Surveillance), Angel Fire and the Gorgon Stare,[8] all named for mythical creatures with supernatural visual abilities. These systems, which are known as Wide Area Persistent Surveillance, consist of arrays of cameras on drones that record video of large areas, allowing material to be reviewed, rewound and fast forwarded so the exact location of suspects can be tracked live. A gentler namesake of the mythological Argus is Argos, another satellite system, launched in 1978 as a climate and ocean-modelling project that was expanded for wildlife tracking in the 1990s. Birds, marine animals and land mammals around the globe wear collars or chips that allow the Argos system to track their migrations. Rather than being designed to monitor enemy forces and criminal suspects, this network uses machine vision to interpret the needs of animals so that governments can better protect them. For instance, seeing the actual paths taken by migrating species allows us to make highway overpasses for animals that are in places where they will actually use them.[9]

In religion, seeing is often, but not always, equated with knowledge, and yet, even when knowledge is set in opposition to sight, the two tend to be connected. In Norse mythology, Odin sacrificed an eye so that he could drink of the fountain of knowledge. Even this was not enough, though: Odin yearned to know still more. The knowledge he wanted could not be gained intellectually or visually, but only through pain: by piercing himself with his spear and by hanging himself from the tree Yggdrasil for nine days. Contemporary humans have the same issue. We can *see* time-lapse videos of melting glaciers but may still be able to keep an emotional distance and put the dangers of climate change out of mind. Sight is a sense that can allow us some distance. Although we are visually immersed in our surroundings, we can always close our eyes and refuse to engage with what we see. We can't do that with our other senses. You can put your hands over your ears, but that won't block out all the sound. You can spit out something that tastes bad, but the taste won't instantly disappear. You may learn strategies to help cope with pain, but you can't shut your eyes and make it go away. Vision gives us access to information but not necessarily to knowledge.

Another example of the opposition between sight and true knowledge is found in the Christian story of doubting Thomas, who does not believe the other disciples when they tell him that Jesus died and came back to life: 'The other disciples therefore said unto him, We have seen the Lord. But he said unto them, Except I shall see in his hands the print of the nails, and put my finger into the print of the nails, and thrust my hand into his side, I will not believe.'[10] Thomas needs to see and touch Jesus' wounds to believe it is really him. After allowing Thomas to touch his wound, Jesus states that those who believe *without* seeing shall be blessed. The rather striking visual image of Thomas placing his finger in Jesus' wound was common in Christian art from at least the sixth century onwards. Caravaggio's version of this motif, painted in 1601, is one of the most famous, showing Thomas's finger deeply inserted into the pale and bloodless wound on Jesus' chest.

Even though knowledge for Odin and Thomas is presented as being most truly achieved through bodily sensation or blind faith, both stories circle around the visual. Odin sacrificed an *eye*, not a finger or an ear, and Thomas's touching the wound is one of the most well-known *visual* motifs in Christian art. Vision and knowledge are deeply connected in Western culture and frequently connect to the divine. In Oak Park and many other American towns, people ask smart surveillance systems to watch over them. As I discussed in the introduction to this book, Donna Haraway insists that this 'infinite vision' is a 'god trick', an impossibility – but that does not stop us longing for it.

Invisible watchers and the modern panopticon

In *Gods and Robots*, Adrienne Mayor argues that Argus, whose full Greek name was Argus Panoptes, or Argus the all-seeing, was an inspiration for Jeremy Bentham's eighteenth-century idea of the *panopticon*, a prison where guards in a central tower could see all the prisoners at all times.[11] The panopticon was a circular prison with an observation tower at the centre and prison cells all around, so a guard at the centre could see all the cells and their inmates from a single vantage point. The side of the cell that faces the centre is barred to prevent escape but otherwise open, so prisoners can always be seen by the guard. The prisoners know there is a guard watching them, but the guard could be anyone. Jeremy Bentham proposed the panopticon in 1785, and in the 1970s Michel Foucault argued that Bentham's design was a model for late twentieth-century society.[12] Foucault argued that societies in the late twentieth century disciplined citizens in the same way as the panopticon disciplined its prisoners. Earlier societies used physical force to make people behave, using brutal and public whippings and beheadings to show individuals what would happen to them if they misbehaved. By the end of the twentieth century, discipline was less about externalised spectacle and more internalised in each individual. Nonetheless, Foucault argued, it has as much power to discipline the population as the violence of earlier times. As in Bentham's panopticon, people in the late twentieth century knew anything they did *might* be seen, so they adapted their behaviour accordingly. They internalised the discipline that the government wanted. In their book *Facial Recognition*, Mark Andrejevic and Neil Selwyn argue that today's smart surveillance is the opposite of twentieth-century panoptic surveillance. In a panoptic society, surveillance is visible. People behave because they know they *could* be watched at any time. In today's society, surveillance is often hidden. When people *are* being watched all the time there is no need to make them aware of it.[13] Traditional CCTV surveillance cameras were often designed to be visible, the assumption being that people would behave better if they knew they were being watched. Corner stores had signs showing pictures of cameras or eyes or slogans such as 'Smile, you're on camera!' Today's automated systems are more likely to be hidden. Flock's automated licence plate reader system relies on cameras that are designed to blend in, and Ring's doorbell cameras are small and unassuming.

The invisibility of smart surveillance also contrasts traditional social visual control. In a comparison of historical African reciprocal, communal surveillance with the modern panopticon, South African philosopher Pascah Mungwini notes that 'in indigenous shame cultures the panoptic gaze is exercised by venerable individuals in one's life as both mortals and immortals, whereas the panoptic gaze provided by modern technologies is largely anonymous and faceless.'[14] The moral censure of people who are significant to you 'can never compare to that posed by a machine manned by somebody almost unknown or unrelated to the perpetrator,' Mungwini continues. Emotionally this may well be true. I would be more upset if a close friend disapproved of something I had done than if a random stranger saw me doing that same thing. Mungwini analyses this as a difference between historical culture and technological surveillance. In many cases, however, I see a continuity from the historical concepts of a gaze from a god or venerable individuals to a conception of technology as having the power to protect the good and punish the wicked. The omniscience of the gods and the jailers has been delegated to machines.

Neighbourhood cameras

Oak Park's drive to buy automated licence plate readers was a response to a shoot-out between two cars speeding down a residential street just after midnight on 7 November 2021. A couple of days later, a local news website published video of the shooting from a neighbour's Ring doorbell camera.[15] The video shows a view of a quiet, dark street, partly obscured by white porch pillars. A car drives by. Gun shots can be heard. A few seconds later, two more cars drive past, the gun shots louder.

The video is surprisingly tame for a 'running gun battle', as the police described it to the *Chicago Tribune* on 12 November. The cars don't seem to be driving particularly fast. But, in a way, the ordinariness of the video makes it all the more chilling. Imagine waking at midnight to the sound of gunshots outside your home and, in the morning, you see a grainy video of your street on one of the local Facebook groups or on the news. Imagine you find a bullet case in the wall of your house, as three neighbours did. Of course you would be scared. I have come to see this fear as a key contributor in the assemblages of which surveillance cameras are part in the United States.

After the shooting, a group of neighbours held meetings and organised a campaign to improve safety. They suggested several actions which the village of Oak Park could take.

One idea was to put speed bumps on the roads and create cul-de-sacs to make it more difficult to speed through the neighbourhood. Interestingly enough, from the point of view of a technology researcher like me, physically building speed bumps or changing road patterns to improve safety would require lengthy governmental approval processes. Installing surveillance cameras, on the other hand, could be done quickly and without much bureaucracy, because surveillance cameras are not heavily regulated in the United States. So, a few months later, the Oak Park police asked the village board for approval to purchase twenty automated licence plate readers from Flock Safety.

Oak Park's Village Board[16] meets most Monday evenings. On 21 March 2022, the main topic for discussion was whether or not to implement Flock Safety's cameras in Oak Park. The village manager started the discussion with a presentation on why the police department wanted to purchase the system. 'Basically, what this is', he explained, 'is an objective platform to identify vehicles and licence plates. It does not identify individuals.'[17] The Flock cameras might not have stopped the shootout from happening, the argument went, but, had the cars' licence plate numbers been captured, the chances of catching the perpetrators would have increased.

The word *objective* is repeated throughout Flock's marketing material and website. This dream that machine vision and data-driven policing will give us objective knowledge is prominent in technologists' and politicians' promotion of the technology. Media scholar Mark Andrejevic calls this 'framelessness' – the idea that objectivity can be achieved by representing the world in its entirety.[18] Considering the same idea from their fields of art history and visual studies, Max Liljefors and Allen Feldman note a similar effect but call it the 'pointless view'. The 'pointless view' lacks the specific point of view we know from conventional images, where there is usually a clear position from which whatever is represented is seen.[19] This is Haraway's 'god trick' again, the idea that knowledge or vision can ever be total and not situated. When we are scared and don't feel we can trust that we are safe, we long for that god trick. The illusion that it is possible – not for us, but for someone or something – to see the world objectively is comforting. We hope that surveillance cameras can provide benevolent omniscient care. Or, at least, some of us do.

Flock cameras as domesticated dragnet surveillance

Flock Safety was founded in 2017 by Garrett Langley, an engineer who was the victim of crime himself and was frustrated by the lack of evidence available to the police. Police had already been using automated licence plate recognition for years at this point, but Flock's innovation was to provide much cheaper cameras that were marketed to neighbourhood associations and individual residents as much as to law enforcement agencies.[20] Their cameras also allowed users to search by several characteristics in addition to the licence plate number, such as the colour and make of the car or features such as whether the car had a roof rack or was dented. By the time Oak Park started debating whether to install the cameras in early 2022, Flock had cameras in more than 1,500 cities in the United States, registering a billion cars a year, and the company was growing fast.

Automated licence plate readers are a form of dragnet surveillance: they gather data about everybody instead of only targeting suspects. This is a major shift in how law enforcement works, and the speed of the shift is astounding.[21] In *Predict and Surveil*, an ethnography of how the LAPD uses technology, big data and machine learning, Sarah Brayne notes that, while directed surveillance of specific targets merely *amplifies* prior surveillance practices, dragnet surveillance 'is associated with fundamental transformations in police activity'.[22] There has been little public debate about the very rapid spread of surveillance in the United States. Oak Park's resistance to the Flock cameras was unusual. One reason for the lack of debate is that the decisions to use surveillance are decentralised. The spread of surveillance happens neighbourhood by neighbourhood, and most neighbourhoods and village boards are small and do not have very active political debates.[23] Another reason is the spread of smart surveillance in homes. You don't even need to buy a new camera to use smart surveillance at home. You can subscribe to online services such as Watchman Scout, which will analyse video from a home surveillance camera and alert you if a car drives past with a licence plate matching an entry on your watchlist.[24] For a slightly higher monthly fee you get more information: a log of all cars that pass, for instance, or a log including the colour and make of each car.

Flock Safety's system is not simply a surveillance camera, it is a network of cameras combined with software that uses image recognition and machine learning to identify certain kinds of behaviour. The promotional material doesn't describe machine learning beyond what is used for image recognition, but the data produced by the system will be connected with other datasets and can be shared with other police departments. Some of these departments will use systems such as the data analytics platform Palantir to combine multiple data sources and use machine learning algorithms for predictive policing. And while Flock Safety is relatively simple, there are other systems, such as Rekor,[25] which combine ALPRs (automated license plate readers) with complex machine learning not just for law enforcement but for city planning and crisis management as well.

Flock's marketing strategy is to domesticate surveillance technology. While most of their competitors target law enforcement, Flock caters to a mixed market of families and police departments and emphasises how ALPRs protect families and children. Comparing the websites and promotional material of these companies shows this difference starkly. Companies aimed more at governments and law enforcement, such as Vigilant or Rekor, use dark blues and a corporate, serious style, whereas Flock uses brightly coloured photos of children, big headings and logos in green and purple, and a promise to 'Reduce crime in your community by up to 70%.' Vigilant is a name that sets you on edge and perhaps too obviously plays on fear, whereas Flock Safety emphasises the safety of the 'flock': the community itself. The cameras you can choose between are named for birds as well: the entry level Sparrow and the Falcon, which has faster upload speed and can send instant alerts to law enforcement. The Raven detects audio and recognises sounds such as gunshots, screeching tyres or a window breaking. TALON is the Total Analytics Law Officer Network, which connects cameras from different municipalities and communities, providing law enforcement officers with more and more data the more cameras connect to the network. The idea of birds as all-seeing is clearly a strong influence on surveillance systems, even systems such as these that are land-based and not, like drones, airborne. An earlier system, apparently no longer an active participant in the market, is named Odin Technologies. Its logo features a raven perched atop the O in Odin, referencing birds again: the mythological ravens Hugin and Munin that brought Odin news from all over the world.

Flock cameras don't look like surveillance cameras. They are elegant black cylinders with a lens near the top, fastened to poles or building walls. Some have solar panels angled jauntily above them, while others run on batteries. A video published on YouTube by Flock Safety shows an official from a neighbourhood near Memphis talk about how well Flock cameras fit into his city: 'It's a subtle presence. It's not something that's going to be an eyesore. . . . It makes you feel safer but doesn't take away from the beauty around you.'[26] The producers' choice to include a clip showing a neighbourhood watch sign threatening that 'All suspicious persons and activities are *immediately* reported to our sheriff's department' is an interesting contrast to this bucolic speech from the commissioner. 'We look out for each other,' the sign says in little letters at the bottom.

Disagreements about the value of surveillance cameras aren't always divided by racial lines, as they seemed to be in Oak Park. Here it was groups fighting for racial equality who were most sceptical of the Flock cameras and white and Asian trustees on the village board who voted for it. In a fascinating analysis of the east side of Charleston in South Carolina, Sarah Koellner describes a very different case, where a church with a majority black congregation ran a fund-raiser to buy Ring doorbells to protect the community.[27] There had been an increase in shootings in the neighbourhood, though there were still extremely few in comparison to the number of shootings in Chicago. The pastor, Matthew Rivers, who is African American, explained: 'We decided to say OK, what can we do then. And that was to raise funds to be able to give families cameras so that we ourselves as a community can police ourselves and help reduce crime in the neighborhood.'[28] They ended up buying 125 doorbell cameras for residents. In this assemblage, surveillance technology was not forced on the community; they chose to use it. It would be interesting to see whether this assemblage works differently to those where neighbourhood surveillance is installed by law enforcement rather than by the community. Does the community retain control over it?

Oak Park: how local history played into the assemblage

Although the Oak Park village board did finally vote to buy the cameras, the board was split 3/3, with the president casting the seventh and deciding vote, while stating that the decision was difficult. Her compromise was that the village should install eight cameras instead of the twenty initially proposed. Most towns adopt Flock Safety's technology with no debate. Oak Park was different for many reasons: its well-educated citizens, the progressive politics of many, and, importantly, the town's legacy of trying since the 1960s to work against racist structures.

Oak Park is a town just outside the Chicago city limit that is known for being socially liberal, diverse and relatively well off, despite its being adjacent to some of the most crime-ridden neighbourhoods in the state. Frank Lloyd Wright grew up in Oak Park and designed many of the houses on the wide tree-lined avenues that criss-cross the town in a regular grid. Ernest Hemingway, another Oak Park native, is often quoted as having described it as a place of 'broad lawns and narrow minds', although nobody has been able to pin down a reliable source for the alleged quote. In 2022 the front lawns of Oak Park homes sported signs with slogans that don't seem to match the narrowness Hemingway once saw: 'Hate has no home here.' 'Black Lives Matter.' 'Injustice anywhere is a threat to justice everywhere.' 'We stand with Ukraine.' Yard signs declare less ideological allegiances as well. 'A Girl Scout lives here.' 'A high school graduate lives here.' 'A member of the local dance team (or middle school basketball team) lives here.' 'Please don't let your dog poop on the flowers.' Other, smaller signs declare the surveillance system used by the house: 'Protected by Xfinity Home, . . . by SimpliSafe, . . . by ADT, . . . by Ring.'

By the time the Flock Camera debate began, I had been living in Oak Park for nearly three months. My husband and I were both visiting scholars at the University of Chicago and took the Green Line from Oak Park to the university a few times a week. Walking along the tree-lined streets I'd always noticed the yard signs, but now I started looking more carefully at the porches to see whether they had Ring doorbell cameras like the one that had captured the video of the cars in the November shooting. On some stretches of street, almost every door had a shiny black Ring, with its silently gleaming eye. Other streets had hardly any cameras. Overall, I'd guess maybe a fifth of the houses I walked past in the neighbourhood had Ring cameras. I stopped to photograph a door with a Ring, then realised it would probably send its owner a video of me photographing it. How strange that every step I take might be watched, not only by the people I can see but by cameras on every door, algorithmically tagging me as an unfamiliar face and as a loiterer, questioning why I was spending a suspicious amount of time looking back at the camera.

Even before we moved here, I had heard of Oak Park's reputation for being progressive and for its systematic work for diversity and equality.[29] As I learned more about the local history, I was taken aback at the extent of the racism that work was trying to overcome. I learned about slavery and the civil rights movement in school, of course, and I have read a lot of scholarship about racism and technology, but I did not grow up in the United States and I have not experienced racial discrimination myself. The very local stories of Oak Park and its surrounding neighbourhoods were far worse than I had imagined. I need to include some of this history here to explain how central it is in the assemblages of which the Oak Park surveillance cameras are part. A few pages in a book such as this certainly can't give the lived experience of a black person living in Oak Park or neighbouring Austin, but it will hopefully be more useful than simply saying 'there is structural racism.'

Until the 1950s there were almost only white people living in Oak Park and the surrounding neighbourhoods. At the start of the twentieth century, 90 per cent of African Americans lived in the South, but, in what is known as the Great Migration, 6 million of them moved to the Northeast, Midwest and West of the United States. Most moved to large cities, and half a million settled in Chicago. As black families moved into neighbour-hoods, white families tended to move out, often to suburbs further away from the city. That's what's called 'white flight'. Businesses moved away when more black people arrived, and, in the practice called redlining, banks refused to finance mortgages in 'risky' neighbourhoods.

The Oak Park River Forest History Museum has a permanent exhibition about this period, with many shocking stories. When Percy Julian, a black chemist who pioneered synthetising medicines and hormones, and his wife Anna Johnson Julian, a sociologist, moved to Oak Park in 1951, their home was firebombed twice, and there were many other racist incidents that are shocking to read about today. Fortunately, many people in Oak Park fought against the discrimination and in 1963 established a Community Relations Commission, which is still in operation, and 'Hundreds Clubs' for each block in 1968 to foster neighbourhood cohesion.[30] Although the Hundreds Clubs no longer formally exist, block parties and shared neighbourhood activities are still a common feature of Oak Park life. People are friendly here.

Oak Park also put legal systems in place to stop discrimination against African Americans. In 1968 a Fair Housing Ordinance was passed. The Housing Center, opened in 1972 and still active today, promotes integration by sending white tenants to vacant units where there are fewer white families and black tenants to units with fewer black families.[31] In addition, 'for sale' signs were banned and are still voluntarily avoided, because white flight was driven by the idea that 'everybody else' was moving, so one 'for sale' sign would tend to lead to more white people moving away. Later, school districts were redrawn to promote diversity[32] and renamed for influential African Americans, such as the poet Gwendolyn Brooks and the chemist whose house had been firebombed, Percy Julian. Even with all this work, the Oak Park police still stop black people on the street six times as often as white people.[33]

The neighbourhoods between Oak Park and the city are among the most violent and the poorest neighbourhoods in the country. Next-door Austin, immediately to the east of Oak Park and part of the city of Chicago, experienced white flight in the mid-twentieth century. First it became a home for middle-class African Americans, but then they moved to the suburbs as crime rose and services in Austin decreased as a result of redlining and other racist practices: 78 per cent of people living in Austin today are African American, 15 per cent are Hispanic and only 5 per cent are white; 39 per cent of households earn less than $25,000 a year, and 64 per cent earn less than $50,000 a year. 30 per cent of Austin residents have no internet access. In Oak Park, 48 per cent of households earn more than $100,000 a year; 70 per cent of adults have at least a four-year college degree; 17 per cent of the population is African American and 66 per cent is white.[34]

Oak Park's history and cultural context helps explain why the Flock cameras were so hotly debated there rather than being implemented without discussion, as in so many other US neighbourhoods. The extreme inequality between Oak Park and neighbouring communities is an important factor in understanding how automated surveillance cameras are implemented. This extreme inequality between neighbourhoods is not at all unique to Oak Park but is a foundation of US society, based on racist systems perpetuated over generations.[35]

Ring doorbell videos and communal fear

The Flock Safety cameras add a layer of surveillance to a neighbourhood that already has thousands of surveillance cameras. Oak Park, like many other neighbourhoods, is inundated by Ring doorbell cameras. Press the doorbell on a Ring, and the homeowner gets an alert on their phone and can see and talk with the visitor before letting them in. With a Ring Protect monthly subscription, owners can use their Ring as a smart surveillance camera that will record any person who gets close to the door and send alerts to the owner. Ring is owned by Amazon, which also provides the app Neighbors by Ring for people to share news about local crime and lost pets. Neighbors integrates with Ring cameras, allowing users to easily upload videos that may or may not show package theft, a person trying to open car doors in a parking lot in the middle of the night, or a suspicious looking person approaching a porch door and then leaving. Neighbors by Ring is only available in the United States, although Ring doorbells may be obtained in many countries.

Rahim Kurwa, a criminologist and sociologist who researches race, policing and residential segregation, argues that apps such as Neighbors are a form of 'social policing' used to build a digitally gated community that disproportionately targets black residents as 'suspicious' and thus supports the white preference for segregation that continues to this day.[36] This is the same 'digital redlining' argument used against automated licence plate readers.

The first video I saw when I installed the Neighbors app on my phone showed a carjacking. The video (recorded on a Ring Video Doorbell 3 Plus, the app tells me) shows a view of the street from a porch with two narrow arches. A car is parked by the kerb at the end of the path from the porch, and a woman carrying something that may be a baby in a car seat walks away from it, followed by a man in a red vest. The man walks slowly but threateningly towards her, pointing something at her that could be a gun, though it is impossible to tell from the grainy video. We hear another man yelling, his voice close to the camera's microphone, perhaps standing in the doorway of his house: 'Oy! Get the fuck away' – the fear clear in his voice. On one side a person who looks like a young teen runs anxiously backwards and forwards. The woman and her pursuer disappear behind a post that obscures them from view, then the man in the red vest runs back out towards the car, opens the door and gets into the driver's seat. The woman and teen back away, re-entering the field of view, and the man, presumably the father of this family, yells 'Get inside!' It isn't until several days later I think to look at where the video was recorded and realise it wasn't in Oak Park at all, but several miles away from our house.

The video is disturbing to watch, and the many comments on the post combine horror at what has happened, concern for the family, and concern for their own safety. 'Where exactly was this?' is a repeated question. People want to know how close they were to danger. 'Thank you for informing us . . . thank goodness the family is ok . . . but can you confirm what streets this took place on,' one neighbour writes. Several people say that they worry about the trauma the incident must have caused the family. Others note how scared they are about how common incidents like this have become: 'What a scary world we are living in. You just can't be careful enough because it can happen under any circumstances.' Another neighbour comments: 'You can't even leave your house without someone trying to rob or carjack you!' This is a level of fear I had not imagined existing here. As I read, I realise that people's fear of this kind of crime actually stops them living their lives in the way they would like. One woman writes: 'This right here is why I don't leave the house with my babies without my husband.'[37]

After years of decline, crime has been on the rise in Chicago since the start of the pandemic, as in the United States overall. It feels very different here from when my husband, kids and I spent a semester in nearby Wicker Park in 2014. Back then, the L, as Chicago's iconic elevated trains are called, was full of commuters and other travellers, and often there was standing room only. I don't remember feeling scared on public transport. In 2022 the carriages on the Green Line, which runs from Oak Park to the University of Chicago and beyond, are almost empty except for homeless people sleeping or smoking. I can pass through the gates to the station without speaking to anyone, without looking anyone in the eye or seeing a smiling face. I don't have to buy a ticket: I just hold my watch to the gate for it to automatically dock $2.50 off my transit account. Maybe I'll try to smile at the transit worker sitting in the booth by the entrance, darkened glass hiding their face from the few people travelling. They rarely look up to meet my gaze. There are surveillance cameras on every platform and in every carriage of the L. But there are no visible conductors or drivers of the trains,[38] and I only rarely saw security guards or other staff on platforms.

It is impossible to be objective when a person you love is a victim of crime. My mind churned over all the ways the assault on my husband could have been far worse. I was furious at the other people on the platform who didn't help. I was angry at the Chicago Transit Authority (the CTA) and the city of Chicago and the world in general for creating a situation where human conductors and drivers have been replaced by surveillance cameras that silently record without intervening. At the same time I was reading voraciously about smart surveillance and how it is promoted as a solution to all this.

Statistics show violent crime is increasing rapidly on public transport and everywhere else in Chicago. I spent hours looking at the datasets published by the city of Chicago, using their online tools to create visualisations of every crime committed on a CTA platform. Data visualisations are themselves a way of seeing the world that prioritise certain kinds of knowledge: data, numbers, deviations from the norm, but not the stories of individuals or the reasons why the numbers increase or decrease.[39] Data visualisations are a kind of machine vision, a way of representing the world visually based on data. They are also decontextualised and sanitised – numbers in neat columns, or pretty coloured graphs on a screen, not the lived experience of violence. News searches gave me stories to go with the numbers. The day after my husband's assault, a customer assistant got into an argument with a traveller, the newspaper reported, and as the man walked away the customer assistant drew a gun and shot him three times.[40] Most startling was a story from just a few months earlier: a University of Chicago student was killed by a stray bullet while taking the L from the university. He would have boarded the train at the same station as we did on our commute home.[41] I was starting to understand that Americans drive not simply because it's convenient, but to stay safe.

Once I started to pay attention to it, I saw fear everywhere I went. At the supermarket, the friendly Hispanic man helping me to pack my groceries asked about the *refleks* fastened to my bag. I explained that it's a reflective strip that I put around my wrist when it's dark so that it's easier for drivers to see me walking. 'In Norway, we all wear these,' I cheerfully explain. 'Oh, we don't walk after dark around here!' he said, looking quite concerned for me. 'You want to be careful!' At that point, I was scared of taking the L, but it genuinely hadn't occurred to me to worry while walking on well-lit Oak Park streets after sunset. A couple of days later, I ate lunch at a café. The women at the table next to me were chatting loudly about some out-of-town visitors one of them was expecting, and, primed as I now was to listen for fear, I took note of the horror in their voices at the idea that the visitors might ride the L to get from downtown Chicago to Oak Park: 'She said she'd seen we lived right near a station so she'd take the L!' The other woman gasped, as her friend continued: 'Well, I told her she was crazy, please take an Uber!'

Everyone wants to feel safe. I understand why people who feel as if they can't safely walk outside at 8 pm, or take public transport, might feel that surveillance cameras are a worthwhile price to pay to regain some freedom. When we're scared and technology firms tell us that they can keep us safer, it's not surprising that people buy into it. Living in Chicago for a few months, I realise that fear of crime doesn't only make people feel unsafe and reduce their trust in their community and government, it also limits people's freedom of movement.

Unfortunately, there is no evidence that the trade-off works. Surveillance isn't reducing crime in the USA. I'll return to that later on, but first we need to understand better how surveillance is seen as a solution.

Surveillance as a promise of safety

Seeing a video of your neighbour having their car stolen at gunpoint right outside their house is frightening, and the Neighbors app makes every video feel close even if the incident actually happened miles away. Most of the comments on the carjacking post were sympathetic or expressed horror or fear, but one suggests a solution: 'This is why we need cameras on every block.' The day before, the Oak Park Village Board had decided to install Flock cameras. Emotions ran high in the public statements read to the board on 21 March, and many of the statements referenced frightening stories to illustrate their fears, stories about situations where a culprit could have been held responsible if only Flock cameras had been installed: the drive-by shootout on 7 November, and a child riding their bike to school when they were knocked over by a reckless driver who didn't stop and will never be held responsible.

Others told stories that positioned the Flock cameras as a threat instead of as a saviour. Several people mentioned a story that had been on the national news, about an African American family in Colorado that was stopped by police because the Flock system had incorrectly identified their car as being on a list of stolen vehicles. The police pulled the family out of the car at gunpoint. A widely circulated video shot by a bystander showed the four children lying face down on the black asphalt. The two oldest have their hands cuffed behind their backs. You can hear them crying, wailing, 'I want my father, I want to go home!' The littlest one, a six-year-old with bright pink braids, leans up on her hands, trying to understand what is going on.[42]

The debate about Flock in Oak Park was driven by residents who were scared and who wanted to feel safer both in their homes and in their neighbourhood. Flock promised to provide that safety. Yet when the Oak Park village manager presented the solution to the board, he carefully stated that Flock was not intended to deter or prevent crime; it would be only an investigative tool.[43] The tool would not be used for traffic violations or making sure people stop at stop signs; it would be used only in situations when drivers were involved in crimes, he assured the board. Most Oak Park residents presumably do not see themselves as likely to commit a crime, but many, if not most, will have got a ticket at some point for not stopping at a red light, parking in the wrong place or driving a little too fast. Reassuring people that Flock cameras wouldn't be used to police these things strengthened the idea that they were to catch outsiders, not Oak Parkers.

People who disagreed with the idea of the cameras argued both that they would make them *less* safe and that it was unnecessarily costly and took attention away from other solutions that would do more to prevent crime, such as making it more difficult to drive fast by changing the roads. Adding cul-de-sacs, stop signs and speed bumps would be more effective ways of reducing the risk of people driving in off the expressway and having a shootout in an otherwise peaceful Oak Park street. Many of the public comments read to the board on 21 March argued that black and brown people in particular would be made less safe by the Flock licence readers, because they are the people who are at greater risk when stopped by the police.

The most common argument *against* automated surveillance technologies such as the Flock cameras or facial recognition is the risk of misidentification that leads to wrongful arrests or individuals being stopped or questioned by police unnecessarily. I don't believe that anyone in Oak Park wants surveillance because they are deliberately racist. They simply want to stay safe in a society with deep-rooted problems and hope that surveillance will help stop crime. But, as Ruha Benjamin writes in *Race after Technology*, racism 'is not only a symptom or outcome, but a precondition for the fabrication of such technologies.' Racism, she contends, is 'not just an ideology or history, but . . . a set of technologies that generate patterns of social relations, and these become Black-boxed as natural, inevitable, automatic.'[44]

Racism exists in all countries, but it plays out in different ways in different places. There is a common assumption that the United States is a tech leader because it has excellent researchers, a strong start-up culture and lax privacy regulations. The USA has clearly gone a lot further than Europe in terms of predictive policing and covering the nation with smart surveillance cameras. An important actor in the assemblage that drives the spread and technological development of smart surveillance is, tragically, the inequity between neighbourhoods that is caused by the country's racist past. Ruha Benjamin might say this racism is encoded in Flock Safety's cameras. Perhaps it is. Perhaps the technology could be used differently if in a different assemblage – if we took the cameras and dashboards and alerts out of Oak Park and Chicago and put them in Bergen or London or Nairobi. Or perhaps the particularly US brand of racism stays part of the assemblage and shifts to the new location, supplemented by local fears and inequalities.

Machine vision situations as affective assemblages

Capsule stories such as these are *machine vision situations*: events or scenes involving machine vision technologies as an agent. The Ring doorbell camera automatically recorded the shootout on 9 November and made it possible for the homeowner to share the video with neighbours and news sites, increasing anxiety about safety in their neighbourhood. There are many other agents in this assemblage in addition to the doorbell camera: bullet casings, cars, guns, frightened residents, and the drivers of the cars who perhaps chose to fight in a quiet neighbourhood street instead of on the expressway because of the cameras there. Assemblages are fluid, with different agents coming into focus depending on how we tell the story. The situation that started the Flock camera debates was the actual shootout and the neighbours' experiences of it. There is also the imaginary situation: the version of this story, imagined by the neighbours who lobbied the village board to buy the cameras, where Flock cameras had already been installed. The cameras would have identified the cars. Maybe, if the cars were stolen, the police would have been alerted in time to stop the shootout from ever happening. If not, the police would have had the information they needed to make arrests and put the drivers behind bars. Perhaps they are right, and the shooters would have been arrested. Weighing that possibility up against the possibilities of false arrests is not an easy task.

I spent time in the previous chapters analysing machine vision as assemblages. A technology can have very different roles and agency when participating in different assemblages. Machine vision situations are assemblages, but when we retell them we tend to use familiar narrative structures. There is often a villain and a saviour, a crisis and a hoped-for resolution. The stories about the shootout in Oak Park feature the Flock cameras as potential saviours, helpers that will enable a resolution of the crisis. In the story of the Colorado children handcuffed and face down on the asphalt, the Flock cameras play the role as villain, not saviour. The technology misidentified the family's car. The police officers followed their district guidelines to treat all stops of stolen vehicles as high-risk situations where suspects should be handcuffed.

Does machine vision reduce crime?

The only real argument for using automated licence plate readers is that they will make neighbourhoods safer by reducing crime and helping to solve incidents. Unfortunately, there is very little evidence that this kind of surveillance really does help reduce or solve crime.

Automated systems such as Flock Safety are relatively new, and there is not a lot of systematic research on them yet. However, traditional CCTV cameras have been used for security and in policing for decades. A systematic review of forty years of research studies on CCTV surveillance up to 2017 led by Eric L. Piza, an associate professor at John Jay College of Criminal Justice in New York, identified seventy-six research studies on CCTV's effect on crime published in 2017 or earlier.[45] Taken together, the studies show a modest but statistically significant reduction in crime, but only for certain types and locations, and only when combined with other forms of active intervention, such as increased or more targeted police patrols, community outreach, or even better lighting. Piza and his team found that vehicle and property crimes were reduced by around 14 per cent and drug-related crime by 26 per cent, but they found no significant effect for violent crime or disorder. They also note that studies of CCTV in the United States did *not* find a reduction in any type of crime. They speculate that this could be because CCTV surveillance was not as often combined with active intervention in the US studies as it was in other parts of the world.

We don't yet have forty years of research on how automated systems such as Flock affect crime, and Piza and his colleagues specify that none of the studies they found discussed automated detection systems. It is possible that automated and immediate alerts to law enforcement will make it easier to provide the active intervention that Piza and his team found reduced crimes. This requires more human resources, though – more police officers or social workers who can respond to the automated alerts. Machine vision alone won't solve the problem. And, as I'll discuss, automated systems have a high number of false alerts, leading to unnecessary police encounters that can be traumatic for innocent people, and also wasting time for police officers.

Other smart surveillance systems are also in use in the Chicago area, but unfortunately data does not show them being very effective. ShotSpotter is used by the Chicago Police Department to automatically detect the sound of gunshots and immediately alert the police. This is machine hearing, not machine vision, but, like ALPRs, ShotSpotter combines dragnet surveillance and massive data gathering with machine learning algorithms to identify suspicious events – gunshots or a stolen vehicle – in real time and send automated alerts to the police. The ShotSpotter website calls the system a 'Precision Policing Platform™', noting that it is 'highly data-driven'.[46] However, as with ALPRs, there are many false alerts. A study by the MacArthur Justice Center found that 86 per cent of ShotSpotter deployments of police officers in Chicago turn up no crime at all, resulting in more than sixty unnecessary deployments of officers every day.[47] The City of Chicago's inspector general released a report in 2021 citing similar numbers, together with the additional finding that 'the introduction of ShotSpotter technology in Chicago has changed the way some CPD members perceive and interact with individuals present in areas where ShotSpotter alerts are frequent.'[48] It was found that the police had begun to stop and pat down people who were in a place known often to generate ShotSpotter alerts, even when there had been no alert.[49] There have also been serious cases of wrongful arrest based on ShotSpotter evidence, including one where a man was imprisoned for a year on a charge of murder before being released due to a lack of any evidence beyond the ShotSpotter data.[50]

But maybe ShotSpotter still reduces gun violence overall? Unfortunately, it doesn't seem to. A national study comparing homicide rates from 1999 to 2016 in locations where ShotSpotter was or was not used found the technology had 'no significant impact on firearm-related homicides or arrest outcomes'.[51] A 2018 partially randomised study had a similar finding: the technology resulted in more than twice as many gunshot reports, but there was no significant difference in the number of confirmed shootings. This meant there was an increased workload for police officers who had to investigate more alerts, but with no gain in terms of identification or investigation of incidents.[52] Despite the lacklustre results from both national studies and Chicago's own data, Chicago's mayor at the time, Lori Lightfoot, renewed the city's contract with ShotSpotter for another two years just a few weeks after receiving the very critical report from the inspector general. The belief in data is strong. Even the inspector general's report, which found that the available data did not clearly show that the value of ShotSpotter outweighed its costs,[53] concluded by saying that perhaps the data isn't good enough and that, with *more* data that improves 'the ability to match ShotSpotter to other police records', we may find that ShotSpotter is actually effective.

Why would we think machine vision technologies such as Flock's cameras will work differently from ShotSpotter? If you believe that cameras deter crime, it follows that, if most places are heavily surveilled, a place *without* cameras would attract crime. This argument was put forwards by Illinois police when they installed cameras along the I-290 expressway that cuts through Oak Park. 'They threaten one another and they say let's take that out to the expressway,' the Illinois state police director Brendan Kelly told a journalist. It's like duelling, he explained. Criminals choose the expressway for their duels because there are cameras everywhere else.[54] Politicians proudly report on arrests made using information from the cameras, even though expressway shootings continued to increase after the cameras were installed.

Fear and distrust feed the surveillance industry

The desire for objective evidence that we imagine surveillance cameras and machine vision can provide seems particularly strong in a country such as the United States, where people no longer trust each other, or authorities, or the news. I'm used to living in Norway, where people generally trust each other and institutions. People in the United States are well below the global average when it comes to trust, and, since the pandemic, Americans' trust in authorities ranging from scientists to public school principals, to police officers, to journalists, to the military has dropped even further.[55]

People long for surveillance and data-driven policing because they don't trust other humans. This hypothesis is supported by a recent quantitative survey in the United States that found that individuals who distrust other people and institutions are more positive towards AI-driven content moderation, while those with more trust in each other are more likely to trust that content moderation by humans is accurate.[56] I think dataism, that 'belief in the objective quantification and potential tracking of all kinds of human behavior and sociality', to use José van Dijck's words, is stronger in societies where people don't trust each other and don't trust their leaders. The same would go for technological solutionism, the idea that technology can solve societal problems. We *believe* in technology: a return to faith-based religion as our trust in one another fades.

Media exposure to news about crime increases people's fear for their own safety. Study after study has shown this, decade after decade. Although crime rates overall have dropped in the last half century or so, coverage of crime in the media has increased.[57] In Gallup's annual surveys of whether Americans think there is more or less crime than the previous year, the majority almost always answer incorrectly that there is more.[58] Consumption of crime news can lead to trusting other people less. Television news makes people more afraid for their safety than print news, and increased use of social media and alternative online news sources also increases fear. Conversely, people who live in walkable neighbourhoods and chat with their neighbours are less frightened by crime news than others.[59]

It's not just that distrust in other humans increases our belief that technology will keep us safe: there's also a reinforcing cycle where surveillance cameras feed our fear, making us feel less safe, leading us to distrust people even more and to want more surveillance cameras. There is a cycle of interaction between institutional surveillance by law enforcement, the state and corporations and home surveillance set up by individuals.

Do doorbell videos cause fear? Do automated alerts raise our sense of the world being full of threats? The pandemic is obviously an important actor in this. The inconsistency of national guidance meant that people in the United States had less trust in the government's ability to protect them from COVID than those in many other countries. The pandemic also led to less physical interaction among people, with video as an intermediary between us. This lasted much longer in the USA than in Norway, where schools were closed for only a few weeks. In Oak Park, schools operated completely remotely from March through December of 2020 and partially so in the first half of 2021, with kids in school only every second or third week. Did Zoom and Ring doorbells make Oak Park less physically connected, scared of each other's bodies, longing for connection and safety onscreen? Does heightened surveillance increase our desire for yet more surveillance? Do Americans who are scared of COVID and of crime simply feel safer experiencing the world at a distance through their smart cameras?

Surveillance technology in the United States feeds upon and encourages fear and distrust. The sense that there is nothing that can be done to make things better is also a factor. It's understandable, in a country where deep structural change seems insurmountable, that people clutch at things they can actually do. Installing more technology lets us feel that we are actively doing something. Not doing anything leads to numb despair.

Understanding this uniquely American assemblage of surveillance systems, algorithms, fear, distrust, decentralised police departments, racist histories, local activism and tech start-up culture is key to understanding how technology does not work in the same way in every context. If you take Flock Safety's cameras and install them in another context, they will be used differently – and yet some of the influences of the other participants in the assemblage for which they were developed are encoded into them. Just as an animal's vision is highly specialised to serve its specific needs, machine vision's sensory apparatus and processing is designed to serve the needs of the context – or assemblage – it is developed in and for. That assemblage includes the developers and salespeople, not just those using the technology.

Machine vision isn't the main culprit in the increases in crime and distrust in the United States, but it is a very potent agent in an assemblage of profiteering companies, a dead-locked political system, centuries of racism and inequality, and a growing anxiety and distrust in the population. Machine vision and other technologies are also often presented as a solution to the problems, although there is a lack of evidence showing that they help, and many situations in which they may do harm and reduce the trust that communities depend on. But, in a trust vacuum, we need to trust something. So we buy Flock cameras and vote for politicians who promise 'data-driven policing'. We believe in machines because it feels like there is nothing else left to believe in. Enlightenment human-ism moved religion from its previously central place in society. Now we are replacing religion with a new faith in technology.

4

Being Seen:
The Algorithmic Gaze

When was the last time you met someone's gaze? Maybe you passed someone on the street and happened to look into each other's eyes for a moment before walking on? Or perhaps you gazed into the eyes of a good friend or a lover or a child? The reciprocity of seeing and being seen is so crucial to human society that our eyes have evolved not just to *see* in a way that is specifically human but also *to be seen* by other humans. In contrast to other primates, the whites of our eyes are visible, allowing us to see where other humans are looking. Humans can tell if another human is looking into their eyes.[1] If machine vision technologies 'see everything', as I discussed in chapter 3, does this shape our relationship with them, just as seeing and being seen builds relationships between humans? Does machine vision return our gaze? How do different machine vision assemblages see us differently?

The subtitle of this chapter, 'the algorithmic gaze', is a reference to the argument by the cinema theorist Laura Mulvey that cinema supports 'the male gaze'. Mulvey's paper, which was published in 1972, contended that the camera in mainstream cinema takes the perspective of a male voyeur, portraying women as objects to be looked at rather than subjects in their own right.[2] Mulvey's concept has been deeply influential in cinema studies, and the idea of a technological 'gaze' has been taken up by many other theorists. Do the algorithms of contemporary machine vision systems situate humans in a particular way, as Mulvey argued that cinema tended to objectify women? What does it mean to be seen by machine vision?

In chapter 2 we saw how Vertov, Svilova and Kaufman framed the 'kino-eye' as seeing the world in a radically different way from humans. In contrast, Mulvey saw cinema as replicating the 'male gaze' of human patriarchy, where women are expected to be passive objects rather than active subjects. This tension between understanding machine vision as radically non-human and as reifying existing societal biases is also very much present in contemporary debates about technology. Mulvey is of course not really describing a gaze that is innate to all cinema. It would be more correct to say that the male gaze is produced in a certain assemblage where the technologies of cinema are combined with a patriarchal society and the commercial system of big budget Hollywood cinema. When the technologies of cinema are combined with the revolutionary spirit and relative gender equality of the early Soviet Union, we get instead the alien gaze of the kino-eye. As argued in earlier chapters, it is the gaze or the *Umwelt* of the assemblage we need to consider, not just the individual technologies or film directors.

The previous chapter explored the conflicting desires of wanting to be kept safe by smart surveillance and of fearing that the gaze of surveillance cameras will be oppressive, unjust, incorrect, and that it may make us more afraid and less trusting of each other. In this chapter, I discuss other ways machine vision looks back at us. I explore the algorithmic gaze of machine vision through three case studies that examine different ways in which it looks back at us. First, I discuss selfie filters and the ways biometrics and facial recognition algorithms conceive of human faces. Selfies and selfie filters are a very immediate route to experiencing this algorithmic gaze. Using datasets of tens of thousands of photos of human faces, neural networks can be trained to recognise faces, to classify them by characteristics such as gender or age, and to generate new images of potential faces. My second case study explores how machine vision is used to automate grocery shopping, library access and other interactions that formerly required us to interact with other humans. Smart cameras are used to watch us in spaces where previously we would have met other humans. Finally, I explore a fictional example of a benevolent AI dictator, Thunderhead, from Neal Shusterman's young adult series of novels *Scythe* (2016), *Thunderhead* (2018) and *The Toll* (2019). Thunderhead watches over each human on the planet with genuine, loving care.

Normalising faces

Machine learning has a *normalising* effect. It builds a model of the most common patterns in a dataset to make mean-ingful predictions or inferences. It produces stereotypes, not defamiliarizations. When you take a photo on your phone, its AI adjusts the light, colour and contrast to fit the most likely scenario based on its training data. This means that, for example, if you try to take a photo of the orange skies of a Californian wildfire, the camera might correct the colour to be grey.[3] If camera software is trained to take photos of a person only when their eyes are open, but the training dataset included only Caucasian faces, it may fail to take a photo of an Asian person's face because it fails to recognise that their eyes are open.[4] The AI is trained to predict what a photo should look like based on statistic probabilities, and it will adjust any 'abnormalities' to approach this statistically desired image. I'll return to what this normalising effect means below.

While camera software performs many automated adjustments to our photographs without our active intervention,
selfie filters allow us to deliberately play with the ways the
camera sees us. Throughout history, artists and amateur
photographers have used self-portraits to deliberately create
self-representations (as I discussed Frederick Douglass doing
in chapter 1) but also to see themselves *differently* by experimenting with different poses and effects. Artists would pose in
unusual ways or dress up in order to create particular impres-
sions. People pulled faces in photo booths and practised poses
and facial expressions. Magazine articles, online videos and
commercial online classes promise to teach people how to pose
their bodies and smile in order to be as photogenic as possible. I
wrote about this in *Seeing Ourselves through Technology*. Selfie
filters or lenses are where it really gets interesting in terms of
explicitly playing with machine vision, though, because they
bring attention to our interactions with machine vision algorithms. Selfies shared in social media have always been about
communication and interaction. As Paul Frosh wrote in 2015,
the selfie 'says not only "see this, here, now", but also "see me
showing you me." It points to the performance of a communicative action rather than to an object, and is a trace of that
performance.'[5] When you play with a selfie lens you engage in a
performative interaction with machine vision. Then, perhaps,
you send the photo you took to a friend, sharing a trace of that
performance with them.

Selfie filters use the same basic technology as facial recognition systems. The algorithm analyses the image of your face in
real time to find your eyes, eyebrows, nose, mouth and chin
and then maps an altered image to your face. On the one hand,
this is another example of how the same technology can be put
to very different uses, with different effects. The same basic
algorithms can be used to identify suspects in a crime or for
playing around with selfies. On the other hand, selfie filters
might accustom us to biometrics and facial recognition more

broadly. Many apps using filters start by visualising how they identify our facial features, overlaying the image of our face with a grid of lines or dots. This familiarises us with the idea of biometrics and facial analysis and will perhaps make us less likely to object to machine learning in other situations.[6]

Another way selfie lenses and image filters affect us is by normalising our idea of what we should look like. Machine learning algorithms and neural networks look for patterns in the datasets on which they're trained and create a model based on the most common patterns. If a model takes too much notice of unusual cases and outliers, it will be unable to make useful generalisations. This kind of exaggerated attention to detail is described as overfitting and gives a high error rate in the machine learning algorithm. Avoiding overfitting leads to the opposite problem and causes *normalisation*. For instance, we would expect a system trained on images on the internet with English-language captions to be biased in the sense that it will be better at recognising or generating images from Western contexts.[7] The model will also normalise the data. If 80 per cent of the people shown in the training dataset images were white, the model may generate new images where 95 per cent of the people are white, because it has found that white people are 'normal'.

The idea of there even being a 'norm' is less than two centuries old. In his introduction to the *Disability Studies Reader*, Lennard Davis points out how the idea of *not* conforming to a norm depends on the idea that there is a norm or an average and that being normal is desirable. Davis explains that it was not until the 1840s that the words 'normal' and 'normality' were first used in the current sense of 'constituting, conforming to, not deviating or different from, the common type or standard, regular, usual'. The concept of normality emerged from the new fields of demographics and statistics that grew rapidly from the early nineteenth century on. The early Belgian statistician Adolphe Quetelet was a key contributor to what

Davis calls the 'generalized notion of the normal as an impera-
tive'. Quetelet used data visualisations to plot the distribution
of features of military recruits, such as their height, and found
the regular bell curve pattern known in statistics as a normal
distribution. If height is plotted along the x-axis, and the
number of people who are that height is plotted on the y-axis,
you get a curve that looks like an upside-down U or a bell. Just
a few people are very short or very tall, and a lot of people are
more or less the same height as each other.

Quetelet took this one step further by arguing that *l'homme
moyen*, the average man, was the most perfect, and that individuals whose bodies and morals were closest to the average
were superior. For the first time, the definition of beauty and
moral goodness was determined mathematically and statistically rather than by theological laws, artists' renditions or an
individual's preferences.[8] As Lennard Davis notes, 'the average then paradoxically becomes a kind of ideal, a position to
be wished.' This privileging of the average is a marked break
from earlier traditions that saw the ideal body, represented for
instance in paintings of Venus, as something 'mytho-poetical',
a 'divine body' that is 'not attainable by a human'.[9]

There is actually no such thing as an average human. In 1952
Gilbert S. Daniels, a US Air Force engineer, sifted through
detailed measurements of 4,063 flying personnel. He started
off by noting that it could be useful to find average ranges for
specific measurements such as height: 90 per cent of the pilots
were between 5 feet 5 inches (165 cm) and 6 feet 1 inch (185 cm)
tall, which is useful to know if you want to decide how tall you
need to make a doorway so that most people don't have to bow
their head to walk through it. For making clothes or designing
an aeroplane cockpit, though, you need to consider more than
just height, and this is where it gets tricky. Daniels chose ten
measurements that are useful for making clothes: height, chest
circumference, sleeve length, and so on. He then checked to
see how many men fell within the middle 30 per cent range

for all measurements. The fall off was sharp: 1,055 men were of approximately average height, but only 302 also had average chest circumference, and, of these, only 143 had average sleeve length, and so on. By the time Daniels reached the ninth measurement, thigh circumference, only two of the original 4,063 men were left, and neither of them had average crotch length, the tenth measurement. Even without descending as far as to measuring crotch length, the data clearly shows the diversity of human bodies.[10] None of us is truly average. We are *all* outliers.

Machine learning models are based on statistics, though, and so they emphasise the norm, not outliers and details. This often leads to what computer scientists call *bias amplification*. In this sense, all machine learning systems can be called normalising machines. Mushon Zer-Aviv's art installation *The Normalizing Machine*, which I mentioned in chapter 1, takes photographs of the exhibition visitors and dissects each photo, assessing how 'normal' each facial feature is as compared to those of the other visitors. *The Normalizing Machine* directly references the work of nineteenth-century anthropometrics, particularly Bertillon's system for categorising criminals based on photographs of their faces and measurements of their bodies. Another artwork that explores and critiques the normalising effect of machine learning is Jake Elwes's *Zizi – Queering the Dataset*. In this work, Elwes took an existing dataset of faces and added 1,000 images of drag queens and overtly genderqueer people and used machine learning to train a model that would generate new, 'queered' faces.[11] While Zer-Aviv's work enacts the normalisation processes of machine learning in order to critique it, Elwes actively alters the dataset to queer the model and demonstrate how machine learning could be designed differently. For everyday users of selfie filters who play with apps that make their faces more 'beautiful', this normalisation can be experienced as racist, gender-excluding and sexualising.[12] Luckily there are also filters that push back against these ideals.

Datasets of faces are frequently used in machine vision to train models that recognise faces or generate new faces. CelebFaces is a dataset consisting of over 200,000 photographs of celebrities' faces. In the annotated version of this dataset, CelebA, each image is annotated with forty binary attributes.[13] The first photo I see when I begin to explore the dataset shows an unnamed woman with closed eyes and perfect makeup pouting her lips as though to kiss someone. The attribute '5_o_clock_shadow' is FALSE, presumably meaning that the face has no beard stubble. Big_lips is TRUE, Attractive is TRUE, and Male is FALSE.

It's easy to see that many if not most of these attributes can't really be slotted into a binary TRUE or FALSE. Gender, for instance, is not a simple binary in real life, with male and female as the only options. In the CelebFaces dataset, male is the default gender. A woman – or, I suppose, a genderqueer or non-binary person – is simply not male (Male = FALSE). Some attributes, such as whether or not the person is wearing glasses or whether or not they have five o'clock stubble, are easier to see as having binary TRUE/FALSE answers. Others, such as Attractive, are disturbing both for the lack of context (attractive to whom?) and the presumption that an individual either is or is not attractive. Yet datasets such as this are what contemporary facial recognition is based on.

Digital computers have been designed around binaries since the 1940s, and binaries are so much easier to compute than richer data that they have remained with us. When we developed the Database of Machine Vision in Art, Games and Narratives, we tried to avoid simple binaries and used richer sets of qualitative tags instead. But when the time came to analyse the data, I found myself wishing for more simple binaries – they would have been so much easier to analyse! They would also have been so much further from the actual stories and movies and artworks and games we were trying to represent in the dataset.[14]

Emotion recognition is another way machine vision sees and acknowledges our faces. In her book on biometrics, Kelly Gates wrote that 'facial recognition technology treats the face as an index of identity, disregarding its expressive capacity and communicative role in social interaction.' Emotion recognition, on the other hand, focuses on that expressive capacity but, in Gates's words, 'treats those affective dimensions as objects for precise measurement and computation'.[15] Software is commercially available today that claims to interpret the emotional state of a person based on a visual analysis of the expressions on their face, despite research clearly showing that there is in fact no direct correspondence between facial expressions and emotion.[16] Affectiva is one such company, and a simple version of its software can be tried out for free by downloading their app AffdexMe. The app's icon is a bright pink background with a smiley face emoticon in white :). When I open the app, I see my face, just as when I open Snapchat – but, while Snapchat encourages me to record my face, augment it with selfie lenses and filters, and then send it to others, AffdexMe wants to interpret my face and tell me how I feel. White dots appear to mark my eyebrows, eyes, nose, mouth and chin, with a white rectangular box drawn to show the part of my face that is being analysed: from my eyebrows to my chin. When I raise my eyebrows, the box expands to follow. I look impassively at my own face and notice the emotions listed at the top of the screen, with percentage bars beneath each word: sadness, smirk, contempt, joy, disgust. Apparently, my resting face looks sad to the app, because a green bar under sadness marks me as being 28 per cent sad. The other emotions are at 0 per cent. I try smiling and achieve 100 per cent joy quite easily. Lessening my smile means that my emotion score drifts down to 66 per cent joy and then switches to disgust. The app uses emojis to annotate my image as well. I have an emoji of a woman's face indicating that the app has gendered me as female. I try to figure out how to make the app register certain emotions: a scrunched-up nose is interpreted as disgust, a crooked smile as a smirk; a single lifted eyebrow seems not to affect anything. The app does not seem to differentiate between what feels to me like a genuine smile and what feels like a fake, sceptical smile. Both register as joy. When I ask my kids and friends to try out the app, they do the same as me, trying out which expressions it can read and then trying to 'break' its readings by making it misread emotions that a human would know were not sincere.

This urge to play with the algorithm is familiar to anyone who has played with selfie lenses on Snapchat or other apps – and to anyone who has visited a hall of mirrors, where you see yourself outrageously tall and skinny in some mirrors and very short and squat in others. But while the alteration apps make you look different to yourself, AffdexMe tells you how a machine sees you – or how it might be seeing you. The white dots show to what aspects of your face the machine pays attention, converting them and their positions to data. The percentage bars tell you how it translates their positions to an assertion about you. You are 30 per cent joyful. You are smirking. You are 72 per cent sad.

Our facial expressions are no longer only ways of communicating emotion to other humans or involuntary expressions of fear or joy, or even identity markers, as Kelly Gates noted. The way we move our eyebrows and nose and mouth are now also ways of manipulating an interface. You can learn to make the computer think you are joyful, or sad, or disgusted by moving your facial muscles in certain ways. Actors have always trained themselves to do this. Perhaps most people do, a little: studying our faces in the mirror as we try out different expressions to see how we look, how others might see us. Social media scholars often cite the work of the sociologist Erving Goffman on how self-presentation is a kind of performance. We are conscious of how we present ourselves to other people, Goffman argues. This deliberate presentation of self is our 'frontstage' performance. We relax our front in private ('backstage', to follow Goffman's theatrical metaphor) and may also show different fronts in different contexts – at work or with a group of friends, for instance.[17] Facial expressions are part of this social performance. Selfie lenses and apps that respond to our facial expressions are reminders that now we perform not only for other humans but for machine vision as well.

Emotion recognition software could be used as a tool to control people's thoughts or, at least, to control their expression of their thoughts. Imagine a dictator wanting to weed out disloyal subjects. He might install cameras and analyse the faces in a crowd, giving his guards or police force orders to arrest anybody whose facial expressions betrayed disloyalty: a smirk or a nose wrinkled in disgusted during a particularly uplifting part of the dictator's speech, for instance, or a look of boredom or disinterest.

In China, emotion recognition systems have been implemented in some schools, prisons and public spaces.[18] These keep track of whether students are paying attention in class and of what they are doing: reading, writing, talking, sleeping. Parents are sent automatically generated reports each day: your child wasn't paying attention for 7 per cent of the day, against a class average of 3 per cent inattention. Other uses appear less draconian. For instance, job recruiters ask applicants to record videos of themselves and use emotion recognition to filter out the applicants that appear insecure or not sincere enough. There are many other possible scenarios. Some might seem useful but could have unintended effects. Would you want your nanny cam to alert you when your child's carer appeared to be depressed, or bored, or angry?[19] Would you want to work as a nanny if you knew that a frown would send an alert to your employer?

When we use selfie filters to see ourselves differently, we interact deliberately with machine vision. Facial recognition in airports or emotion recognition in schools is not something the individual can control. In these cases, we adapt to the knowledge of this algorithmic gaze. In both cases, the algorithms have a normalising effect. Selfie filters that beautify your face by smoothing your skin or making it more symmetrical remind you what you are 'supposed' to look like and how you deviate from this norm.[20] Emotion recognition can make us act in the way we think the algorithms expect, adjusting our facial expression to what we assume to be a normal expression.

So far in this chapter I've talked about quite intimate interactions with machine vision. Taking a selfie or playing with filters is usually something done in private or in a small group of friends. You might share the selfie, but the actual interaction with the machine vision is between you and the machine. When I take a selfie, I smile and pout and pose for the camera, knowing I will delete most of the images I capture. Only the machine sees me like this. The machine vision algorithms of my phone are a collaborator whose ways I learn so I can make my photos look the way I feel. Often I fail and give up in disgust, frustrated that machine vision doesn't see me the way I want to be seen.

There are far more public settings where machine vision looks back at us and shows us how it sees us. One example is the way supermarkets and libraries are using surveillance cameras and, sometimes, facial recognition to replace service workers. In these cases, machine vision isn't shaping our self-identity but providing access to a facility to a privileged group. In the following I'll explore how unstaffed supermarkets can integrate machine vision technologies into very different assemblages with quite different effects, comparing small Norwegian supermarkets to Amazon Fresh stores in the United States.

The assemblage of an unstaffed grocery store

Fewer than 100 people live on Tansøy, an island off the west coast of Norway. The local grocery store has been run by the same family for four generations. The owner used to open up the shop for only a few hours a day. But in June 2022 the store was 'digitised' and is now open all day as a self-service, unstaffed shop. Customers scan their bank card to enter and use self-checkout machines when they leave. Surveillance cameras fastened to the ceiling keep watch, and if a customer needs help they can initiate a conversation with the owner (who keeps an eye on the shop through an app on his phone); if the owner is unavailable, customers can talk to people at a remote service centre who can monitor the cameras in the Tansøy shop, as well as other shops in the network. The owner is thrilled with the new set-up, according to an interview on Mat-Norge's blog. Now he can go fishing without worrying about having to stay in the shop in case any customers come. Mat-Norge's system launched in 2019 and is used by dozens of small grocery stores in rural Norway.[21]

In the United States, the digital mega-company Amazon is also experimenting with machine vision in grocery stores, but in a very different way. Amazon's 'Just Walk Out' technology[22] consists of a dense network of surveillance cameras with image recognition software that observes when a shopper removes an item from a shelf and automatically adds it to their purchases. Shoppers scan an app when entering, and, as they do so, facial recognition is used to identify their face so they are tracked throughout the shop. Amazon sells the technology but also uses it in its flagship Amazon Fresh grocery stores, which have opened in big cities around the United States.

One morning I found a flyer on our doorstep in Oak Park announcing that a new Amazon Fresh store was opening nearby. I wanted to see the surveillance system, so of course I went. The North Riverside Amazon Fresh is at the end of a huge parking lot surrounded by big stores. To my surprise, the shop was fully staffed. In fact, I think I saw more employees staffing the fresh food sections, greeting customers and restocking shelves than I do when shopping at Whole Foods, a traditional grocery chain bought by Amazon in 2017. When I walked in, a friendly young man greeted me and explained I needed to scan a QR code in my Amazon app to enter, and again to exit, and the cameras would take care of the rest. I was a little disappointed that it wasn't all facial recognition, but I suppose Amazon didn't actually have a photo of my face connected to my account before that day.

I scanned my app and walked in, looking up to see a network of grey scaffolding hanging from the ceiling, with hundreds of small black cameras hanging down from metre-long poles. The cameras were all identical and shaped almost like birds. Their black, rectangular 'faces' slanted back from a protruding vertical line that reminded me of a nose or beak. On each side was a white and black 'eye': a round black camera lens surrounded by a white square. These bird-like cameras gazed silently down at me as I walked through the vegetable section. I wondered whether they were intentionally designed to look like birds. The thicket of cameras is definitely not intended to blend in or be discreet. Amazon wants you to know you are being watched. The anthropomorphic or zoomorphic design of the camera-birds is a way of making the intense surveillance seem a little friendlier. The technology is on display as something we as shoppers are expected to find cool and enticing, not threatening or dystopian. This may not work entirely as intended. A study of the system found that customers liked the convenience and not having to stand in line but also reported 'a sense of embarrassment and doubt due to tracking and the over-control generated'.[23]

Each piece of fruit was priced individually so the cameras could count them. Even the bananas were rather comically separated from their bunches and placed neatly beside each other, barely touching to make them maximally visible for the cameras. The wine and beer section was cordoned off and guarded by a friendly staff member. He said he had to check my physical ID to allow me to enter. When I had filled up my cart with bananas, milk and a bottle of wine, I scanned my app again to walk through the exit gates. My receipt, with a list of all my purchases, arrived in my Amazon app an hour later.

Technically, the system seemed to work well. Like all the journalists who have written about Amazon Fresh, I tried to test the system by picking up items and replacing them on the shelf. When my receipt arrived in my Amazon app only one item I'd put back had been billed to me. It felt strange to click 'return' on an item I hadn't carried out of the shop, but my money was refunded without any fuss.

If we imagine an Amazon Fresh store as an organism, what would its *Umwelt* be? Its most obvious sensors are those bird-like cameras and the entrance and exit gates where it connects facial images to established customer identities. It has a map of the shop, and its image recognition systems have clearly been trained to recognise bananas, milk cartons and wine bottles. It knows where items are supposed to be located. The store knows which customers are inside it at any time because of the gates where people scan in and out, so the facial recognition systems have to differentiate between only a small number of people. The store's systems just have to recognise the person who takes an item from a shelf and add the item to the correct person's list of purchases.

If we zoom out and imagine the Amazon corporation as the organism instead of just considering the individual Amazon Fresh store, the *Umwelt* becomes a lot bigger and a lot more unsettling. The bird-like cameras and the store itself become a sensory input device for Amazon as a whole, supplementing the corporation's extensive data on individual customers with biometric data about their faces and presumably also gait pattern and other shopping habits. Which vegetables do customers look at but not buy? Are there aisles that a customer never even enters? Do people linger? Do they chat with other customers?

I've been an Amazon customer since the late 1990s, when they were a small start-up allowing me to find out about and purchase books my local bookshops in Norway didn't stock and at the time couldn't order for me. Amazon's business model has changed immensely since then, as the internet has become commercialised and personal data is the currency corporations use to sell us even more, whether consumer goods or ideologies. I am not sure whether Amazon knew what I looked like, how I walk or how I move through a shop before I entered the Amazon Fresh store. They certainly do now. As Anthony McCosker and Rowan Wilken write in *Automating Vision*, the visual data that facial recognition algorithms sense and store is valuable.[24] Perhaps gathering this data about their customers is the main goal of the Amazon Fresh stores? If so, it makes sense to set the stores up in cities and suburbs where Amazon already has very strong reach, with local fulfilment centres and many drivers. If I order something from Amazon in the Chicago area, it can usually be delivered the next day at the latest, and more common items often arrive the same day as I order them. Amazon Prime trucks drive through the streets of Oak Park every day, their drivers dropping parcels off on front porches surveilled by Ring doorbell cameras so the 'porch pirates' won't steal the parcels before the homeowner returns. Amazon owns Ring as well. Perhaps next time I walk past a Ring doorbell camera it will recognise my face and alert Amazon that my coat looks a little worn out and so I might be receptive to an ad for a new one.

Non-commercial institutions also use surveillance cameras. In Norway, libraries started expanding their opening hours to include unstaffed hours as early as 2013, and now many public libraries let people stay after the librarians go home. Patrons have to register specifically to access the library after hours, and, once they are registered, their library cards give them access to the building. Security cameras are installed but are not monitored in real time, and they have no AI analysing the video. Security guards stop by a few times every evening and do a round. According to a special issue of the librarians' trade journal in 2018, there have been hardly any problems. A sofa was damaged once, but that might have happened during regular opening hours, one librarian said. Others report no issues at all.[25]

Scandinavian and Southeast Asian countries have been among the first to open up libraries like this, and high levels of trust are commonly put forward as a reason why the system works in those countries. It's more than just trust, though. In the United States, public libraries are one of the few indoor spaces that welcome everyone, and the many homeless people who live in US cities often use libraries as a safe and warm space, sometimes sleeping in tents set up just outside the library so they can spend all day inside.[26] In countries where everybody has their basic needs covered, libraries don't have to be de facto homeless shelters as they are in the United States. As we saw in chapter 3, poverty and inequality are key participants in machine vision assemblages.

The Norwegian system relies largely on community trust, with the surveillance cameras added on more or less as an extra. As the Tansøy grocery store owner says, 'When you trust your customers, they behave accordingly. We have lots of cameras watching, so you'd have to be a cold fish to steal anything.'[27] The paradoxical combination of trust and surveillance is repeated by other shop owners: 'I don't think people become more dishonest just because they're alone in a shop. And we have cameras to spot any shoplifting,' a manager in Sandnes told a newspaper reporter. I searched Norwegian media for reports of theft from automated unstaffed shops, but the only hit was about a farmer who had set up a roadside fridge with eggs on the honour system, who said about three trays of eggs were taken without being paid for every week, and could people please try to remember to transfer money when they bought eggs.[28] No surveillance cameras or automation were involved. This kind of trust exists in rural parts of the United States as well. When we drove through Indiana, heading back towards Chicago after a camping trip, we stopped at a roadside farm stand. Cobs of corn and other vegetables were laid out on a table, next to a pink plastic basket full of dollar bills. A handwritten sign taped to the basket read 'Money. Make your own change ☺.' No staff or surveillance cameras were needed. There are in fact a few American libraries that use the same system as Danish and Norwegian unstaffed libraries. They are in small towns, not urban areas, and in libraries that would otherwise have been open for only a few days a week. Like the Norwegian grocery stores, surveillance cameras are monitored remotely and a security guard comes by at regular intervals.[29] No facial recognition or other algorithmic systems are used.

The *Umwelt* of the unstaffed library systems is fairly similar in the USA and Norway, depending of course on how many participants we include in our analysis. What does the library assemblage sense? Unique identifiers of library patrons entering the building. Books that are borrowed and returned. The surveillance videos are captured but not automatically processed or stored, although it is easy to imagine that being done. A slightly different question from biosemiotics would be to ask what the library 'organism' *needs* to sense. A tick needs to sense warm blood to find its food. A library has different needs and purposes according to who you ask: the librarian, the politician, the homeless person, the avid reader. The assemblage shifts according to where you stand. However, it can be locked down if a particular set of values, needs or cultural assumptions are encoded into its technological infrastructure. Amazon's 'Just walk out' technology is an example of values being embedded or locked into technology in this way.

Controlling access

A common use of facial recognition is access control. At airports, cameras inspect travellers' faces and scan their passports, checking to see that the live human's face matches the stored image in the databases. If the faces match, the automated gate opens, or the immigration officer is given a green light to let the traveller enter the country. In China, residential apartment buildings use facial recognition instead of keys or keycards. A friend tells me this is a problem when he visits his parents, because his face isn't in the system. It doesn't matter, because the security guard knows him and shows his own face to the camera to open the door so my friend can enter.

Sometimes facial recognition is proposed as a solution to problems that don't really exist. In Australia, for instance, a technology company was given large public grants to develop a system for automated taking of attendance in classrooms. Media scholars Neil Selwyn, Liz Campbell and Mark Andrejevic analysed the implementation of the technology in a paper that uses Madeleine Akrich's script analysis model to tease apart the scripts used to sell the system to schools.[30] The disconnect between the company's pitch to investors and funders and the teachers' experience is striking. The company argued that 'manual attendance tracking is labour-intensive, time-consuming, and prone to circumvention and inaccuracy', and that it wastes time that could be used for learning. However, teachers pointed out that those minutes at the start of class taking attendance aren't just about checking names off a list, they are also about greeting each student, making eye contact and getting a sense of how the students are feeling. This not only allows students to settle into a new class period, it also builds relationships and gives the teacher information that helps them adapt the lesson to the students' needs. For a school kid, being seen and acknowledged by the teacher is important.

In the UK, some schools started using facial recognition on kids in lunch queues to verify which students had paid for their lunch. The system was faster and more hygienic than other systems, the technology company argued, achieving 'an average serving time of five seconds per pupil'.[31] Speed is apparently a strong sales argument for new technologies. But, in many cases, technology masks other solutions. If a 25-minute break isn't long enough to serve all the students lunch, perhaps those breaks should be longer? As we saw in chapter 3's discussions of the call for 'data-driven policing', technologies are sold as easy solutions. The tech companies attempt to *inscribe* a set of possible actions into the technology, such as speedy lunch queues or effortless registration of attendance. Real-world settings are rarely that simple, though. In Madeleine Akrich's terminology, the technology is *de-scribed* in the 'confrontation between technical objects and their users', when the 'user's real environment is in part specified by the introduction of a new piece of equipment.'[32] In the Australian classrooms, the technology removed an opportunity for casual but meaningful interaction between teachers and students. In addition, teachers had to troubleshoot, reboot and manage the technology. In the lunch queues, facial recognition technology allowed students to avoid interacting with the staff. In this particular case, after criticism by the UK's Information Commissioner's Office, the schools stopped using facial recognition and went back to their old system, where students punched in a PIN code to make a purchase.

The use of machine vision to remove points of social interaction is particularly concerning in societies where trust and community are eroding. Fleeting encounters with strangers are integral to feeling part of a community when you live in a city, so removing these encounters is the last thing we should do if we want to live in safe, robust communities. Such encounters involve more than the 'civil inattention' that the sociologist Erving Goffman wrote about in the 1970s. Civil inattention describes the way we negotiate strangers in big cities, by non-verbally acknowledging their presence while giving them privacy by not engaging in conversation.[33] Christine Bigby and Ilan Wiesel write about the importance of 'convivial encounters' with strangers where some conversation occurs, as well as 'moments of everyday recognition'.[34] We should design our schools and cities and technologies to support these encounters.

Watched by benevolent AI

My last examples are from fiction and express the comfort of feeling seen and looked after by technology. Although many stories position AI as a slave to humanity, AI and robots are also often given protective, custodial roles in science fiction. In 1967, as computers were becoming more visible in our culture, Richard Brautigan wrote the poem 'All Watched Over by Machines of Loving Grace', dreamily describing an idyllic coexistence:

> a cybernetic meadow
> where mammals and computers
> live together in mutually
> programming harmony
> like pure water
> touching clear sky.[35]

We could call this technological ecology, a term James Bridle uses in *Ways of Being* to express the need to see technologies as part of our ecology, in constant interaction with other species.[36] It is also a poetic description of a world where humans participate in an assemblage with machines, other mammals, the sky, water and trees. Although most of Brautigan's poem describes a world where the boundaries between nature and technology are collapsed, the last stanza suggests a dream of technology having a more protective and actively caring role, as humans are returned to our 'mammal brothers and sisters' and we are 'all watched over / by machines of loving grace'.

The young adult novel series *Arc of the Scythe* (2016–19) by the American author Neal Shusterman presents a contemporary example of a benevolent AI that cares for humans. In this future, death has been eradicated, and the Thunderhead, the AI, organises everything for the best for all humans, using an extensive surveillance system to keep watch and make adjustments to help each individual. This world has conflict and corruption, but caused by humans, not by the Thunderhead. To keep population numbers at a sustainable level, a group of people are designated Scythes who are tasked with killing people. The teenage protagonists have been recruited as Scythes and are taught the ethics of the system, but of course there are corrupt Scythes as well. Because the scything system was designed partly to keep a check on the AI government, the Thunderhead cannot intervene in its business but still manages to come up with a way to collaborate indirectly with our teen heroes to save humanity. Despite the rather too frequent ghoulish killings in the first book, the depiction of the Thunderhead as a genuinely caring AI is fascinating. It speaks to a shift in society where AI and machine vision have become integral parts of our world. Many uses of surveillance are deeply problematic, as we have seen throughout this book. And yet there is more and more surveillance in society. Chapter 3 explored how fear and machine vision can be intertwined. Thunderhead and Brautigan express a different emotional response to machine vision: safety, care, love and hope.

The second book, *Thunderhead*, includes the Thunderhead's diary notes, which are placed between chapters narrating the adventures of the teenage Scythes and other key characters. The Thunderhead sees its observation as care, not surveillance: 'It is important to understand that my perpetual observation of humanity is not surveillance. Surveillance implies motive, suspicion, and ultimately, judgment. None of these things are part of my observational algorithms. I observe for one reason, and one reason only: to be of the greatest possible service to each individual in my care.'[37] The vast majority of people appreciate the Thunderhead's care. A few groups do not, so the Thunderhead has alternatives for them. For instance, they can choose to live in the Charter Region of Texas, which has no cameras in private homes and where people can drive their own cars if they so wish.

The Thunderhead explicitly compares people's trust in it to the human tendency to believe in omnivoyant gods:

> Perpetual observation is nothing new: It was a basic tenet of religious faith since the early days of civilization. Throughout history, most faiths believed in an Almighty who sees not just what humans do, but can peer into their very souls. Such observational skills engendered great love and devotion from people. Yet am I not quantifiably more benevolent than the various versions of God? I have never brought about a flood, or destroyed entire cities as punishment for their iniquity. I have never sent armies to conquer in my name. In fact, I have never killed, or even harmed a single human being. Therefore, although I do not require devotion, am I not deserving of it?[38]

This benevolent surveillance and protection is what people dream of when entrusting their homes to Ring doorbell cameras and their neighbourhoods to automated surveillance systems. Of course, we don't take it quite this far, and I have not yet seen a serious suggestion that we give up democracy entirely to an AI.

In the book series, the Thunderhead's world is portrayed as almost utopic, except for the corruption of the Scythes. The happy ending involves the Thunderhead successfully creating new benevolent AIs that can launch humanity into space, allowing the population to continue to grow beyond the limits of what Earth can sustain. This apparent success does come with an unsettling undertone. The Thunderhead is loving, yes, but also rather arrogant, and this society seems to render human autonomy impossible. There is nothing to fight for because everything is perfect.

The Thunderhead's loving surveillance is similar to that of parents watching over their children. Keeping an eye on your kids is absolutely necessary when they are small and dependent on you for everything. As they grow older, they need more freedom and independence. There is plenty of technology to help with parental surveillance, ranging from baby monitors to GPS tracking on phones or smartwatches.[39] The ubiquity of these technologies may well be extending the length of time parents attempt to keep watch over their children. Ring doorbell cameras are used not only to surveil outsiders who might threaten the home but also to keep track of teenagers sneaking in and out of the house and trying to avoid their parents' attention. The book series' theme of teenagers coming of age in a world controlled by a well-meaning but controlling AI might seem rather familiar to a teenager growing up today.[40]

I did not grow up in a world where benevolent surveillance beyond early childhood was considered a good idea. Quite the opposite: my parents, teachers and popular media drilled into me the dangers of totalitarian state surveillance. My parents' generation was born during or shortly after the Second World War, and the Cold War was in full swing during my childhood and adolescence in the 1970s and 1980s. My family moved from Australia to Norway in the late 1970s, and as I grew older teachers told us more about their experiences of the war in Bergen under Nazi occupation. I learned that databases of people could be dangerous. Norway shamefully didn't allow Jewish people to enter the country until 1851, and at the start of the war there were only around 2,100 Jews in Norway. In 1942, the Nazis required all Jews to be registered with the police and to have a red letter J stamped in their identity papers. A few months later, 773 Norwegian Jews were deported and sent to concentration camps. Only thirty-five survived.[41]

There were no surveillance cameras in Nazi-occupied Norway. However, the Nazis used detailed data collected about the population to oppress, torture and murder people. Finding that the most recent census, from 1930, was out of date, they set up a comprehensive population register with continuously updated addresses for each resident in towns over a certain size. In their proposal for the new law, the German police were quite honest about their goals in setting up the registers: 'The current situation urgently requires close surveillance of the movements of people in Norway.'[42]

I turned thirteen in 1984, and that year I read George Orwell's dystopian classic *Nineteen Eighty-Four*. I was horrified at the idea that people's every move might be watched. In high-school social studies classes, we learned about the Stasi in East Germany and their networks of spies and immense collections of data about individual citizens. I read Margaret Atwood's *The Handmaid's Tale* and was shocked at the realisation that changing a few lines of computer code in centralised systems could instantly stop all women's bank cards and key cards from working. Technology and data aren't evil in themselves, but they can make it a lot easier to set up a dictatorship.

Despite this suspicion of surveillance, I was also brought up in a society with very high levels of trust in government. Given the Norwegian population's lacklustre support for the Jews during the Second World War, this trust seems built at least in part on a system that historically has looked away when harm was done to minorities. Norway was a very homogeneous society until the 1970s and a relatively poor country until oil was discovered in the late 1960s. It only gained its independence in 1905 after more than five centuries of being ruled by Denmark and then Sweden. This meant there was no established nobility or ruling class, as power had been held in

Denmark and then Sweden. Twentieth-century Norway had a strong emphasis on equality and fairness. The social welfare systems put in place after the Second World War went hand in hand with a sense of *dugnad*, a tradition of helping each other and working together that can be traced back to old Norse times. I find myself loving the ease of the Norwegian system, where my bank ID gets me access to everything from prescriptions to banking. I don't have to fill out a form to pay my taxes or renew my passport; I just check the pre-filled info is correct and confirm it. I can almost see how people might love the Thunderhead.

The assemblage of being seen

The examples I've discussed in this chapter can all be seen as assemblages of technologies, humans and cultures that have their own specific *Umwelt*s. These *Umwelt*s are focused on seeing us, on seeing humans. Machine learning models that identify and classify human faces are trained on datasets that may or may not be biased, and, because of the way machine learning works, they have a normalising effect, rendering minorities and outliers less visible and teaching us what we are supposed to look like. These models are complex and often difficult to understand, and the historical biases of their datasets are encoded into them. Unstaffed supermarkets and libraries can be implemented with very little or no AI, as in the case of the rural Norwegian stores, or with thickets of cameras armed with image recognition software to identify both shoppers and the items they buy. The *Umwelt*s of these two alternative assemblages are very different from each other. An Amazon Fresh shop is like the sensory apparatus of a far larger organism, sucking up data about its customers to be added to the extensive data already stored by Amazon's systems. The Thunderhead is a fictional example of a benevolent AI that sees everything on Earth. It has chosen not to have a body, remaining 'pure' software, but it admits that it has stationary cameras and roving camera-bots throughout the world. The cameras are not its body: they 'are nothing more than rudimentary sensory organs', Thunderhead explains, continuing, 'The irony, however, is that with no body, the world itself becomes my body.'[43] A system like Amazon is not that different from Thunderhead. It has sensory organs in homes (Ring and Alexa), in supermarkets (Amazon Fresh), in delivery trucks that roam the streets, in Kindles and phone apps, on television screens (Amazon Prime Video) and of course on its website, serving and tracking its millions of customers. Only some of these are visual sensors, but, taken together, Amazon's *Umwelt* might be nearly as extensive as Thunderhead's.

Machine vision can't see everything, though. Just like any other organism or assemblage, an assemblage incorporating machine vision evolves or is optimised for certain purposes. Sometimes this means that it does not see us in the way we want to be seen or that it does not see us at all. At other times, it means we can evade it when we do not want to be seen. In the final chapter of this book I will discuss the blind spots of machine vision.

5

Seeing Less:
The Blind Spots of
Machine Vision

There is a scene in Janelle Monáe's *Dirty Computer*[1] that beautifully captures the joy of tricking machine vision. Monáe's character and a friend are driving along a country road in a futuristic red sportscar when they are stopped by a drone that wants to check their identities. The two friends submit to the drone scanning their eyes. But as soon as the drone has flown away, they jump out and open up the boot of the car – and two more people jump out, laughing. All you need to do to trick a retina scan is hide your friends in the boot of your car.

Movies and science fiction stories abound with examples of humans tricking technology. In the movie *Minority Report*, our hero evades the ubiquitous retina-scanning identity trackers by having his retinas replaced by a black-market surgeon and hiding in a cold bathtub so the spiderbots don't sense his body heat. In Cory Doctorow's novel *Little Brother*, the protagonist tricks the gait recognition cameras at his high school by putting gravel in his shoes to change his walk. Video games often require the player to hack surveillance technologies to achieve their goals. This is a major feature of the gameplay in the *Watch Dog* series, where the player can hack into drones and surveillance cameras to see more, to stop others seeing, or to escape being seen. Hacking and altering machine vision is also a persistent theme in digital art.[2]

These stories are retellings of an ancient human story: that of the disadvantaged hero that wins by their wit. The trickster hero, the clever slave: this character is known from ancient times. In Norwegian folktales, the character is Askeladden: the youngest son nobody expects anything of, but in every story his curiosity and cunning allow him to trick the troll and win the princess and half the kingdom, while his more favoured older brothers fail. Polytheistic religions and mythologies tend to have such characters too: lesser gods such as Loki, Hermes or Anansi, who are never fully in charge but who can sometimes outwit the leaders and unexpectedly take control.

The trickster hero is often the representative of those who lack power in a society. *Minority Report*, *Little Brother* and *Dirty Computer* are all stories of people working against oppressive regimes that use technology to suppress dissent. A variant of the trickster narrative occurs when the trickster is punished and firmly placed back in their traditional society role. This often happens with female characters. In a traditionally highly patriarchal society such as the Muslim Middle East, the 'wiles of women' are a common feature of stories, with women portrayed 'as tricksters, masters of deceit, and (importantly) of social risk'.[3] However, the wily women of Arabic stories are often punished and then 'redeemed and rewarded by marriage and motherhood'.[4]

The previous chapters have been about how we see with and are seen by machine vision. This chapter is about *not* being seen. What can machine vision not see? How do people actively evade machine vision? I have started with the trickster hero and will move on through the angry rebel, personified here through Katniss in *The Hunger Games*. I discuss artist hacks and adversarial attacks on machine vision technologies and the failures of machine vision when its biases mean it does not succeed in seeing everyone.

Just as the trickster hero represents those without conventional power, stories about tricking and evading machine vision tend to position the technology in a position where it supports those in power. The machine vision is seen as a participant in an oppressive assemblage – an illegitimate government as in *Dirty Computer*, or a government that has chosen surveillance and control over freedom, as in *Little Brother*. In these stories, tricking machine vision is a way to reclaim agency, whether to have fun and meet friends or to take political action to rebuild a democracy.

In other stories, the protagonists must evade machine vision or be killed. In the first episode of the popular Korean series *Squid Game* (2021), participants play a lethal version of the children's game Red Light, Green Light. If a mechanical doll senses them moving, they are shot dead. Standing completely still when the doll 'looks' at them is the only way to win the game. The players have little agency here; they simply figure out the rules and do what they have to do to stay alive. This is different from the drone scene in *Dirty Computer*. The music video features trickster heroes who do something unexpected. They appear to go along with the expected response when they submit to the drone's identity control, but, once the drone has gone, they merrily retrieve their friends from the boot of the car, making a mockery of the totalitarian state's assumption that it has full control over its population.

The people in *Dirty Computer* are able to trick the drone because they know how it works. This cultural imaginary of algorithms – how people *think* machine vision works – has recently been analysed by scholars as 'folk theories' about AI and algorithms.[5] Basically, people are trying to imagine how the technology sees the world – its *Umwelt*. Sophie Bishop describes how 'algorithmic experts' on YouTube claim to understand how the recommendation algorithms work.[6] If you follow their advice, you can play the algorithm and win in the competition for visibility. Despite the algorithmic experts' attempt to frame their advice as objective, Bishop argues that it is closer to lore than science: 'in practice, algorithmic expertise often takes the form of algorithmic lore: a mix of data-informed assumptions that are weaved into a subjective narrative.' Emily van der Nagel and Ysabel Gerrard analyse the opposite phenomenon, where social media users try to hide their posts from the algorithms so that they will not be censored. Van der Nagel coins the term 'Voldemorting' to describe this, after the *Harry Potter* books where Voldemort is 'he who must not be named'.[7] Gerrard writes about how users wanting to discuss and sometimes promote their eating disorders circumvent content moderation on Instagram, Pinterest and Tumblr.[8]

While early content moderation was mostly based on flagging certain words and hashtags, automated image analysis has become common in recent years. Algorithms identifying nude images or female nipples are used both by social media platforms that do not allow them and by law enforcement agencies that want to stop the spread of photographs of sexual abuse of children. People who legitimately want to share their sexy selfies theorise ways they can beat the nude detection algorithms – for instance, by pasting round stickers next to their breasts to confuse the nipple detection or by wearing fishnet stockings with no underwear so the algorithm doesn't flag the photo for nudity. These strategies are similar to the friends hiding in the boot of the car in *Dirty Computer*: they evade machine vision using trickery rather than a technological hack. The point is to communicate with other humans but keep the message hidden from the machine vision, with its rudimentary visual processing. And, of course, social media companies discover that people are tricking the system and so change their methods to try to stop users 'gaming' the algorithm.

Another strategy that requires more technical know-how is to alter the pixels in the image so subtly that a human will not detect it, but so that it will render the image illegible to a neural network trained for object recognition. This technique was first discovered in 2013, and the results were published in a paper with the understated title 'Intriguing properties of neural networks'.[9] I explained in the introduction that neural networks have layers of units (sometimes called neurons) that each interpret certain information about an image. The information is expressed as a numeric value between 0 and 1. The units in one layer pass on their values to the next layer, which interprets them, assigns new values and passes them on to the next layer in the network. When the scholars discovered that changing a single pixel can change the prediction completely, they realised that it was the relationships between units rather than individual units themselves that held the semantic information. These relationships are referred to as 'vector space'. When a facial recognition model sees a face, it is seeing not eyes and a mouth but relationships or vectors between the different units it is analysing. Those units aren't 'eyes' and 'mouth' but numbers between 0 and 1. Units in the first, or deepest, layer of the network might correspond to 'contrast', 'a horizontal line' or 'the position of an eye', but by the time units have been fed into many more layers and reinterpreted again and again the high-level units have no direct relationship to the image itself. Intriguingly, it is possible to calculate *which* pixels to change in an image so that it is misclassified. This 'intriguing property' of neural networks is not random but a built-in feature.

Since 2013, research into techniques that fool image recognition models has blossomed. If you search for scholarship on almost any kind of image recognition, such as recognising nude images, you will find many articles describing methods for doing it, but also articles describing adversarial techniques for thwarting the algorithms. There will likely also be papers presenting methods for dealing with the attempts to thwart the algorithm. The cycle of method–adversarial attack–new method seems endless. However, the most effective tactics are often those that follow the trickster logic of the four friends in *Dirty Computer*. The easiest way to stop an autonomous vehicle from seeing a stop sign is to not to alter the pixelation of the image but simply to remove the stop sign.[10]

'There are four ways to make something invisible for a camera.' These are the first spoken words in Hito Steyerl's video artwork *How Not to be Seen: A Fucking Didactic Educational .mov File*. 'To remove' is the second of the very simple techniques Steyerl demonstrates: she carries the sign off screen. The rest of the video explores more advanced forms of machine vision. The resolution of a satellite camera is 1 square foot per pixel, so in order not to be seen you need to be smaller than a square foot. The satirical instructions on how not to be seen are both absurd and thought-provoking. Steyerl's work plays upon a Monty Python skit from 1969 that is also titled 'How not to be seen'. The skit is presented as a public service film from the government and shows various people hiding from the camera and then being shot or blown up as soon as they stand up and become visible. Despite its hilarity, it reminds us that, in some regimes, being seen will get you killed.

Breaking the oppressors' tools

Technology and machine vision are often portrayed in science fiction either as saviours or as villains. Superheroes such as Iron Man save the world using technology, but totalitarian dystopias also rely on machine vision, as in the world of *Dirty Computer* or Orwell's *Nineteen Eighty-Four*. In *The Hunger Games*, machine vision is consistently framed as the tool of the oppressors and as a contrast to the honest courage of our hero Katniss. The hunger games themselves are a televised battle to the death. The ubiquitous surveillance cameras and constant televised spectacle are the most prominent machine vision technologies used in the games, but there is also the holographic augmented reality display of the arena that the game masters can monitor, edit and manipulate at will. Other machine vision technologies include the holo in the third book, which projects a holographic map of the Capitol with booby traps marked, and the night vision glasses Katniss finds in the first book. I find the night vision glasses particularly interesting because they are marked as a tool of the oppressor that Katniss reluctantly chooses to use.

Katniss is presented as a very reluctant user of technology throughout the series. She is a hunter who taught herself to shoot with a bow and arrow in the woods outside District 12. The night vision glasses are one of just a few technologies she actually uses herself, apart of course from her bow. At first she thinks they are sunglasses, 'but when I put them on they do something funny to my vision, so I just stuff them back in my pack' (p. 166). Later, Rue explains what they are, and Katniss tries them again in the dark. This time, she is impressed: 'I can see everything from the leaves on the trees to a skunk strolling through the bushes a good fifty feet away. I could kill it from here if I had a mind to. I could kill anyone' (p. 206). However, Katniss never does use the glasses for hunting or killing. Instead, she uses them to hide from 'the Careers', her opponents who also have night vision glasses. She uses machine vision in order *not to be seen.*

The Careers' dependence on technology is presented as a contrast to Katniss's natural hunting abilities. Katniss scathingly thinks of 'the Careers with their night-vision glasses tromping around the woods' (p. 229) with 'their heavy, branch-breaking bodies' (p. 248). When Katniss does use her glasses, it is not to augment her natural senses but to recover a little of what she has lost. After successfully blowing up the Careers' food supply, she is deafened by the sound of the explosion and too weak to run. She hides: 'The first thing I do is dig out my own glasses and put them on, which relaxes me a little, to have at least one of my hunter's senses working' (pp. 225–6). When she wakes up, she is still wearing the glasses, which are rendered useless by daylight: 'When I open my eyes, the world looks slightly fractured, and it takes a minute to realize that the sun must be well up and the glasses fragmenting my vision' (p. 227).

The Hunger Games presents machine vision technologies as generally not to be trusted and as tools of the oppressor, whether the oppressor is the Careers, the game masters or the political regime of the Capitol. Machine vision can sometimes be useful, though, and can be manipulated or subverted by Katniss and the rebels. Katniss uses the holographic map (the holo) for a while, but, like the night vision glasses, its perception is flawed: it fails to show all the traps, and some of her companions are killed. In the end, Katniss ends up using it as a bomb rather than as a visual aid. Most spectacularly, in the second novel, Katniss destroys the technological simulation of the arena by shooting what appears to be the sky with an electrified arrow. By using her bow, a relatively low-tech weapon, Katniss stays true to her basic, non-technological nature. Donna Haraway wrote that the idea that there is a binary opposition between nature and technology is false: we are all cyborgs. Despite Haraway's denial, that binary is still part of our shared imagination. Katniss is more a rebel hero of the people than a trickster, but, like many tricksters, she wins over technological oppression using simple means. She is uncorrupted by technology.

Hiding from facial recognition

Real-world rebels also have strategies for hiding from machine vision. The Occupy movement started in 2011 and was one of the earliest protest movements where participants covered their faces specifically to avoid facial recognition software. It wasn't the first time protesters have hidden their faces. In fact, New York City has an anti-mask law dating all the way back to 1845, instated because of riots where protesters were wearing masks and costumes to disguise their identity. In the twenty-first century, being identified by machine vision is a greater risk to protesters than another human being recognising their face. Today's protesters must assume that the police and political opponents will capture images of their faces and run them through facial recognition databases, attempting to find a match for their identity. Even if their identity is not determined immediately, the images may be used in the future, when better technology and more detailed databases of photographs may enable identification of all participants in a particular protest march.

Artists and activists have developed a range of tools to evade or fool facial recognition and emotion recognition. Adam Harvey's *CV Dazzle* (2010) offers a selection of make-up and hairstyles that make it difficult for machine vision to recognise a human face. The title of the artwork references older forms of camouflage, as the artist explains: 'The name is derived from a type of World War I naval camouflage called Dazzle, which used cubist-inspired designs to break apart the visual continuity of a battleship and conceal its orientation and size. Likewise, CV Dazzle uses avant-garde hairstyling and makeup designs to break apart the continuity of a face.'[11] Leonardo Selvaggio's *YHB Pocket Protest Shield* is a kit made specifically for the #BlackLivesMatter protests in the USA in 2020. The kit aims simultaneously to protect the wearer from COVID infection and from being distinguished by facial recognition systems. It consists of a plastic face shield with round stickers that can be attached it. Selvaggio handed out shields at protests, exhibited them in art exhibitions and also provided an instructional video demonstrating how to make the kit from items you might have at home. A more technologically advanced option is the Reflectacles eyeglasses, which shield the wearer's eyes from infrared light, thus thwarting many kinds of facial recognition. The Reflectacles also have frames that reflect only infrared, and not visible light, so that surveillance cameras show the wearer's head as enveloped in light rather than any details of the face itself. Reportedly, protesters in Hong Kong in 2019 ordered many pairs of these glasses. But, in practice, the protesters mostly wore more easily accessible supplies to block view of their faces: surgical masks, goggles, hoodies and scarves. They also shone pen lasers towards police surveillance cameras, attempting to disrupt the facial recognition software, and knocked down surveillance towers that they thought were connected to a facial recognition system.[12]

Broken machine vision

The difference between human vision and non-human or more-than-human vision is often understood as a distortion. The distortion can be a creative force, as we have seen in examples ranging from the exciting defamiliarisation of the Kinoks' kino-eye to the poignant beauty of Richard Mosse's thermal photographs of migrants. The distortion can be a way of exploring our own reflected images, as with selfie filters or the studio photos of the nineteenth century. But the intended or unintended distortions of machine vision are a major cause of cultural anxieties about new forms of visual technologies. We worry about deepfakes, about not being able to trust what we see, or about the bias and discrimination that exists in facial recognition algorithms that misrecognise women and people with dark skin. We are right to worry about these problems. Machine vision can be used to deceive us, as with deepfakes. There is unintended bias embedded in facial recognition algorithms, which misrecognise dark-skinned people and women far more often than white men. In fiction and games, machine vision is often shown as flawed and not working properly. Sometimes this is advantageous, as the human protagonists can deceive it, as in Janelle Monáe's *Dirty Computer*. At other times, it means that the protagonist's connection to the world is weakened, as when the android Markus in *Detroit: Become Human* struggles to find a new optical unit, and the player sees the world through his faulty vision with jagged red fault lines.

Being misrecognised by an algorithm that insists on interpreting you as male, when you are not, or identifying you as wanting breast enlargements, when you do not, can be jarring. In other cases, machine vision fails to recognise people as humans at all. If facial recognition occasionally doesn't work for you, it might just feel like a minor annoyance. But what if it hardly ever works for you, although it seems to work for everyone else? In *Facial Recognition*, Mark Andrejevic and Neil Selwyn write about 'the low-level attritions, inconveniences, incursions and interruptions that can result from the background use of FRT in social contexts.' They call these inconveniences 'micro-oppressions' and point out that they are more likely to be experienced by people who are already discriminated against or in vulnerable positions.[13] Facial recognition systems in the 2000s and early 2010s often failed to recognise black people at all. The Xbox Kinect gaming system was an example. The Kinect uses gestural interaction, so, in order to play a game, you need to stand in front of the gaming console's camera so that it can recognise your face and begin to analyse your movements. The African American researcher Joy Buolamwini ran into a problem when trying to use the Kinect. It instantly identified her white colleague's face but was completely unresponsive to her own black face. Buolamwini told the story during a TED talk she gave on racial bias in facial recognition algorithms. She showed her audience a video of her standing in front of the game console, which doesn't respond to her at all. She reaches for a plain white face mask, puts it on her face, and the algorithm instantly overlays the image with the biometric grid and allows her to begin to play.[14]

Not being seen by facial recognition can be an advantage if you are hiding from a totalitarian state or participating in protests. But when you want to pass immigration or play a game on the Xbox Kinect, it can feel profoundly disabling not to be recognised by the camera, especially when it is clear that the colour of your skin is the reason that you are denied access. Buolamwini went on to perform audits of facial recognition systems with Timnit Gebru, and they found that major systems were markedly worse at identifying black women than white men.[15] This inaccuracy not only stops black women from playing games, it has also led to false arrests of innocent black men that were incorrectly identified by facial recognition software as being at the site of a crime.[16] As Andrejevic and Selwyn point out, even low rates of inaccuracy mean that the technology fails for a lot of people. They give the example of airports, where facial recognition is beginning to be used for boarding. Cameras scan passenger's faces instead of their boarding cards to verify that they have a ticket for the flight. These systems are advertised as being more than 99 per cent accurate. When thousands of passengers are being scanned, even a 1 per cent failure rate means a lot of people are misrecognised.[17] When facial recognition is used for matters of life and death, such as arrests or even drone strikes targeting an individual, a racially biased failure rate can be castastrophic.

Making bodies machine-readable

Facial recognition renders human bodies visible to an authority by making them machine-readable. As mentioned earlier, using facial recognition to verify a person's identity is relatively easy if the system is just checking that their face matches the biometric details stored in the data in their passport. It is also feasible with limited groups of people, such as the passengers on a single flight or persons who have recently entered an Amazon Fresh supermarket. To search for an individual in a population of millions is far more difficult and would require a lot of processing power.

Those in power have come up with many different ways to make it easier to visually sort people into groups with different rights and privileges. I already mentioned the red letter J stamped in the passports of Jewish people in Norway during the Nazi occupation. In her book *Dark Matters: On the Surveillance of Blackness*, Simone Browne argues that there is a direct link between the letters that were branded on the bodies of enslaved people in the United States in the nineteenth century and the biometric fingerprints and facial data that are used in surveillance today:[18] S for Slave, F for Fugitive, J for Jew. There are so many visual codes for making status immediately legible: uniforms, yellow stars, pink triangles, orange jumpsuits, expensive business suits. There are many visual codes for self-expressed identity too, and these tend to be more flexible with boundaries that are less absolute. Make-up, hairstyles, clothes, the way you walk and move are all ways of expressing or performing identity that can be interpreted both by other humans and by machine vision.

Machines still do better with unambiguous categories, ones and zeroes, not fuzzy nuance. So, governments and institutions make bodies and status machine-readable. During the COVID pandemic, many countries issued QR codes for individuals based on their vaccine status. People had to scan their QR code to enter restaurants or board a flight, and if the scan came up red instead of green you were not given access. Often these techniques involve assigning a unique identifier to an individual body that can be visually confirmed using machine vision. Once a person's identity is verified, more information about them can be retrieved from a database. The biometric data about my face that is stored in my passport and my phone is an example: it makes my face into a living QR code that can be scanned and read by machines. It can be tricked, but it requires technical know-how and a willingness to break the law. Or perhaps it just requires a trickster spirit and a willingness to make the rebellion a public challenge rather than an illicit deed. In 2018 a member of the German art collective Peng! applied for a passport using a photograph that merged an image of herself with an image of the EU commissioner for foreign affairs and security policy. The passport was issued with no questions asked, and presumably either the artist or the commissioner could have travelled using it. Next, the art collective encouraged European citizens to volunteer to merge their passport photos with pictures of Libyan artists to enable them to travel to Europe. Peng! presented this as an art project (titled *Mask.ID*), but, like many activist artists, they were also serious in their critique of the system.[19] In Norway your photo is now taken at the police station when you renew your passport, which puts an effective stop to this particular hack.

The trickster and rebel heroes in this chapter perform a resistance that is crucial for democracy. These stories are imagined, and the uses of machine vision are often far beyond what is actually possible or being done in the real world. Reading and watching and playing these stories about evading machine vision offers a mode of thinking about technology and society that allows us to think about 'what if?' scenarios rather than just responding to what has already happened.

What I like most about these tricks and hacks, though, is their playfulness. They're fun. I love playing a hacker in *Watch Dogs*, bringing down an oppressive regime by hacking cameras and drones. I like the unexpected tricks and surprises of these stories and projects, like Katniss shooting the simulated sky of the arena with her bow and arrow or the artist who merged two photos in her passport. These trickster stories give me hope when I get too gloomy worrying that we'll inevitably drift into a totalitarian surveillance state. That hope is the focus of the conclusion to this book.

Conclusion: Hope

Since I started both thinking and writing about machine vision several years ago, I've had three main questions to which I've wanted to find answers. The first is about agency. Is technology taking over the way we see? The software in my camera now automatically adjusts the photos I take, fixing the contrast and the colours, and even selecting the instant when the person I'm photographing has their eyes open or has the best smile. Does that mean that the software has more control than I do? Working through the many stories and examples in this book, I have come to think of technology as sharing agency with us humans. Smart cameras and other machine vision technologies are participants in assemblages with humans and other agents. In this book I have explored many examples of how technologies work differently in different situations, different contexts, different assemblages. Agency is distributed and complex when it comes to machine vision technologies.

Trust and truth were my second concern. When I started researching machine vision, I thought that knowing about deepfakes and image generation and playing with filters and selfie lenses would make us lose trust in images. I thought machine vision would fit in with ideas about a post-truth society, sitting neatly beside fake news and disinformation to make us stop believing images we see on the news or in social media. Instead, we see an increased trust in many kinds of images. Police departments and politicians in the USA promote 'data-driven policing' and smart surveillance cameras as technological solutions to the American people's loss of trust in institutions. People install doorbell cameras and baby monitors that send alerts to their phones when something happens: an unknown person prowling around their front yard or the baby stirring in the night. It seems that, when human beings lose trust in other people and in institutions, we grasp at technology and trust it all the more.

My third concern was algorithmic bias. Joy Buolamwini and Timnit Gebru have shown how facial recognition algorithms are less accurate for women than for men and for people with dark skin than those with light skin.[1] Often the problem is in the datasets used to train the machine learning algorithms. If a system is trained on photos of white men, it will do a better job at recognising them than at recognising black women. Other sources of bias include false assumptions about what the data means or the normalisation that happens in some kind of machine learning, where the neural networks' search for patterns and similarities means that the most common cases are amplified. This has led to the binary distinction between male and female faces being stronger in generated images than in the actual population or the training data. While there is more awareness of bias now than a few years ago, the problem hasn't been solved.

We are inextricably enmeshed in assemblages with machine vision technologies. Unless we move off the grid, we cannot escape this coexistence with technologies. We change as we participate in an assemblage. But we can also change the other participants in that assemblage. That is where we can nurture hope. Machine vision technologies can foster sympathy and community as well as anxiety and fear.

Machine vision is a *sensing* technology. Rather than thinking of how humans see or how technology sees, it is more useful to think about how we see in more-than-human assemblages. It is not just machine vision that changes how we view the world, it is the assemblage, which can include much more than technologies and humans. It makes a big difference if surveillance technology is implemented as part of Amazon's business model or in a small rural grocery store beside a Norwegian fjord.

I find myself most attracted to the ways that machine vision can help us to see differently from the way we can see on our own. As I discussed in chapter 3, dreams of omnivoyance lead to oppression and fear, and there is no evidence that more surveillance reduces crime. We do know that more exposure to media coverage of crime, especially television news, increases people's fear of crime.

In her book about sympathy and the power of how our emotions influence one another, Jane Bennett argues that fear and anxiety are depoliticising.[2] Keeping a population anxious is one of the best ways to keep it docile. Assemblages that increase anxiety are ideal for totalitarian governments and capitalist monopolies. It seems likely, then, that more home surveillance and sharing of doorbell videos will make people more scared and damage communities. I don't want to try to see like a god. But I do want to expand my human vision and see and understand more ways of being and seeing than I can access with my own two eyes.

Machine vision can open our senses to new ways of seeing that reconnect us to each other or to our environment. Looking into that stone mirror 8,000 years ago must have felt like a miracle. Frederick Douglass had photograph after photograph taken to show the world his face on his own terms. Some selfie filters may push us towards formulaic ideas of beauty we can never live up to, but there are also a host of silly filters that are just fun to play with and which can be used for self-expression and self-discovery. Time-lapse videos can be used to see across timespans that humans can't easily sense and understand on our own, whether it is the migration of forests that James Bridle writes about in *Ways of Being* or the time-lapse selfies I discuss in *Seeing Ourselves through Technology*, where people make videos from years of daily selfies. Video chats with distant loved ones allow us to stay close to people we might otherwise have lost touch with. Art exhibitions and rock concerts use image generation, holograms and other visual technologies in ways that inspire us, that make us marvel and wonder and feel each other's presence. Seeing time lapses of trees growing and glaciers melting or using satellite images to map animal migration are examples of how seeing the world as participants in more-than-human assemblages make us more connected to the world around us and better able to understand other species than we are if we stay limited to our human senses. Machine vision can show us patterns, truth and beauty that we might not have noticed without it.

As I wrote earlier, Rodin argued that the representation of the world shown to us by a photograph is not true, because 'time does not stand still'. But the truth Rodin spoke of was only a human truth. Machine vision can allow us to access more-than-human truths about our world. How can we use this technology to strengthen the bonds between humans and between humans and other species on Earth rather than allowing it to separate us?

Humanities scholars often point out the problems with machine vision, but I also want to focus on hope. Bennett argues that we need to feed our anxiety into anger and sympathy. There is certainly a place for anger. I think there is as much power in sympathy. I love machine vision. I love playing with selfie filters, I love the high-quality photos my phone can take now, and I love our robot vacuum cleaner, which uses machine vision to navigate our house to clean the floors. I am sceptical of sales pitches about emotion recognition for recruitment or attempts to replace human interactions with smart cameras, but I enjoy using FaceID to unlock my phone. Sometimes I am conflicted: I am deeply concerned about the rapid spread of smart surveillance, but I was glad when the person who assaulted someone I love was apprehended because of surveillance footage. I was relieved when my doctor used frequent ultrasounds to reassure me that my third pregnancy was going well after I had had two miscarriages. I am deeply grateful that video chat keeps me close to distant family in ways that were impossible a few decades ago. I love playing video games and exploring virtual reality stories using a VR headset. I love the excitement of being able to experience other ways of seeing than those my own eyes and brain provide. I hope this book won't completely scare you off machine vision but that it will help you think about what kinds of machine vision you want – and do not want – to have in your life and your community. What kinds of assemblage do you want to participate in?

As I finish writing this book, I have uninstalled Neighbors. I don't want to see videos of carjackings any more. Instead of looking at videos of possible crimes, I look through the photos on my phone. I let the algorithm lead me through automatically generated slideshows assembled from photographs the machine vision identifies as similar to each other. The software knows the faces of each of my children and shows me montages of each beloved child growing older year by year. It asks if I would like to see photos taken at the beach or in the snow. There is a slideshow dedicated to a trip with my husband and kids last summer and another of Christmas dinners over the years. Then I open up a video chat and call my mum, happy that this technology I can hold in my hand allows me not only to see myself but to see more, to see at a distance, and to see the people I love.

Notes

Introduction

1 On gender and racial bias, see Buolamwini and Gebru, 'Gender shades'. See, for instance, the model card explaining the bias embedded in DALL-E, a neural network trained on internet images to generate fresh images from written prompts.

2 Mitchell, *Artificial Intelligence: A Guide for Thinking Humans*.

3 See ibid., or Shanthamallu and Spanias, 'Introduction to machine learning'. The first few pages of Bommasani et al., 'On the opportunities and risks of foundation models', also provide a good overview of the history of machine learning and how it works. The GPT models have been particularly influential in text generation. They are trained on vast quantities of text from the web and books and are capable of generating natural language. The paper that introduced GPT-3 was Brown et al., 'Language models are few-shot learners'. The paper that introduced DALL-E, the first image generation model to work in a similar manner, was Ramesh et al., 'Zero-shot text-to-image generation'.

4 Frank Rosenblatt proposed 'the perceptron' in a 1957 report and followed this up with a journal article in 1958. See Rosenblatt, 'The perceptron: a perceiving and recognizing automaton';

Rosenblatt, 'The perceptron: a probabilistic model for information storage and organization in the brain'.

5 See Mitchell, *Artificial Intelligence*, 37.

6 Crawford and Paglen, *Excavating AI*.

7 See Brown et al., 'Language models are few-shot learners'.

8 Bommasani et al., 'On the opportunities and risks of foundation models'.

9 See Mitchell, *Artificial* Intelligence, pp. 191–5, for an explanation of semantic space, which is also called vector space or latent space by others. I also found the explanation of this in McCoy and Ullman, 'A minimal Turing test', p. 2, to be useful.

10 Ramesh et al. explain that DALL-E is trained on 250 million text–images pairs from the internet, including the Conceptual Captions dataset, which is available from Google, and a filtered subset of YFCC100M, which consists of Flickr images with captions. See Ramesh et al., 'Zero-shot text-to-image generation', p. 4, for a description of the training data. The YFCC100M dataset is described in Thomee et al., 'YFCC100M: the new data in multimedia research'. Conceptual Captions can be downloaded from https://ai.google.com/research/ConceptualCaptions/. See also Van Noorden, 'The ethical questions that haunt facial-recognition research', for a discussion of ethical issues relating to using web images to train AI models.

11 The citation is from Goh et al., 'Multimodal neurons in artificial neural networks', which is an online paper that is accessibly written with interactive examples.

12 Mitchell, *Artificial Intelligence*; Crawford, *Atlas of AI*.

13 Haraway, 'Situated knowledges', p. 581.

14 Ibid., p. 582.

15 The artist Richard Mosse's work *Incoming* (2014–17) does this, using military thermal cameras to document migrants entering Europe.

16 Dijck, 'Datafication, dataism and dataveillance', p. 198.

17 Brayne, *Predict and Surveil: Data, Discretion, and the Future of Policing*, p. 55.

18 The research was part of the project Machine Vision in Everyday Life: Playful Interactions with Visual Technologies in Digital Art, Games, Narratives and Social Media, which has received funding from the European Research Council (ERC) under the European Union's Horizon 2020 research and innovation programme (grant agreement No. 771800). For more details about the Machine Vision in Art, Games and Narratives database, see Rettberg et al., 'Representations of machine vision technologies in artworks, games and narratives: documentation of a dataset'.

19 Some of the team's publications include de Seta, '*Huanlian*, or changing faces', and 'APAIC report on the holocode crisis'; Solberg, '(Always) playing the camera: cyborg vision and embodied surveillance in digital games', '"Too easy" or "too much"? (Re)imagining protagonistic empowerment through machine vision in video games', and 'Hologrammer i grenseland: ikke-menneskelige aktørers tilstedeværelse og handlingsrom i spill [Holograms in the borderlands: non-human presence and agency in games]'; Gunderson, 'Populærkulturelle forestillinger av utvidet virkelighet'; Gunderson et al., 'Machine vision creepy-pasta: surveillance devices in digital horror'; Kronman, 'Intuition machines: cognizers in complex human-technical assemblages', 'The deception of an infinite view: exploring machine vision in digital art', and 'Classifying humans: the indirect reverse operativity of machine vision'.

20 The TV series *Black Mirror* was first developed by Channel 4 in Britain and was taken over by Netflix from season 3 onwards. 'The entire history of you' is episode 3 of season 1, written by Brian Welsh and directed by Jesse Armstrong, and first aired on Channel 4 on 18 December 2011. 'Arkangel' was episode 2 of season 4 and was written by Jodie Foster and directed by Charlie Brooker. It was released on Netflix on 29 December 2017.

21 For an analysis of how the player interacts with machine vision in *Watch Dogs*, see Solberg, '(Always) playing the camera: cyborg vision and embodied surveillance in digital games'.

22 See the full list of the games, artworks, movies and novels I mention at the end of the book.

23 Rettberg, 'Situated data analysis'.

24 Paglen, 'Operational images'. Paglen used the term 'operational' rather than Farocki's 'operative'. The two terms are used indiscriminately, though 'operational' has become more common. For a detailed discussion, see Hoel, 'Operative images: inroads to a new paradigm of media theory'.

25 Kurgan, *Close Up at a Distance*, pp. 12–13.

26 Carolyn Kane, in *Chromatic Algorithms: Synthetic Color, Computer Art, and Aesthetics after Code*, presents a media archeological history of synthetic and algorithmic color in video art, digital art and bioart to understand the evolution of color.

27 Kittler, *Optical Media*, p. 226.

28 Bekhta, 'We-narratives: the distinctiveness of collective narration'; Fludernik, 'Let us tell you our story'; Rettberg, '"Nobody is ever alone"'.

Chapter 1 Seeing More

1 Enoch, 'Archeological optics'.

2 For an educational and entertaining description of how animals sense the world, see Yong, *An Immense World: How Animal Senses Reveal the Hidden Realms around Us*.

3 Rettberg, 'Apps as companions: how quantified self apps become our audience and our companions'.

4 Bennett, *Vibrant Matter: A Political Economy of Things*, p. 25.

5 See White, *Medieval Technology and Social Change*. In a harsh review the following year, Sawyer and Hilton accused White of technological determinism and argued that his analysis was incorrect (Sawyer and Hilton, 'Technical determinism: the stirrup and the plough'.) However a more recent article goes a long way towards vindicating White. See Roland, 'Once more into the stirrups'. Langdon Winner's article 'do artifacts have politics?' from 1980 is another classic reference that makes a strong argument for how technological artefacts ranging

from bridges to nuclear power stations determine societal development.

6 Neil Postman introduced the term 'media ecology' in 1970:

> I call the alternative 'media ecology'. Its intention is to study the interaction between people and their communications technology. More particularly, media ecology looks into the matter of how media of communication affect human perception, understanding, feeling, and value; and how our interaction with media facilitates or impedes our chances of survival. The word ecology implies the study of environments: their structure, content, and impact on people. (Postman, 'The reformed English curriculum', p. 161)

See also Strate, *Media Ecology*, for a recent introduction to the field.

7 McLuhan, *Understanding Media*; Hildebrand, *Aerial Play*; Taffel, *Digital Media Ecologies*.

8 Flusser, *Towards a Philosophy of Photography*.

9 For a discussion of cultural and technological filters, see Rettberg, *Seeing Ourselves through Technology*; Rettberg, 'Et algoritmisk blikk', discusses how machine-learning based filters in our cameras combine with recommendation algorithms to prioritise certain kinds of photos.

10 See Conley, 'Apparatus theory, plain and simple', for an introduction to apparatus theory. The male gaze is introduced in Mulvey, 'Visual pleasure and narrative cinema'. Baudry, 'Ideological effects of the basic cinematographic apparatus', is a key reference in apparatus theory.

11 MacKenzie and Wajcman, *The Social Shaping of Technology*, p. 5.

12 'Each plateau can be read starting anywhere and can be related to any other plateau' (Deleuze and Guattari, *A Thousand Plateaus*, p. 22).

13 Hayles, 'Cognitive assemblages: technical agency and human interactions', p. 33.

14 Ibid.

15 Okorafor, *Lagoon*, pp. 116 and 199.

16 Bennett, *Vibrant Matter: A Political Economy of Things*; Braidotti, 'A theoretical framework for the critical posthumanities'; Tsing, *The Mushroom at the End of the World*. In his 2006 book *Assemblage Theory*, Manuel DeLanda proposes a complex structural system of assemblage that he sees as a development of Deleuze and Guattari's work, but which I find too rigid for my needs and so do not draw upon.

17 Bohigian, 'An ancient eye test – using the stars'.

18 Seneca, *Natural Questions*, p. 152.

19 These and other theories are discussed in Sines and Sakellarakis, 'Lenses in antiquity'.

20 Sines and Sakellarakis describe a number of finds of lenses in artisans' workshops and argue that the use of lenses both for fine work and for examining artwork or identifying whether a seal was genuine must have been well established in ancient Greece and Rome. This seems to contradict Kittler, who wrote that Nero was the only person in ancient Rome with access to lenses: apparently, he had emerald glasses for viewing the gladiators at the Colosseum. See *Optical Media*, p. 72.

21 When a group of optometrists and scholars analysed the eyes of the 4,500-year-old statue of the seated scribe, they found that the eyes show remarkable anatomical knowledge for the time, and that the knowledge of optics required to grind the lens was noteworthy. See J. Enoch et al., 'Lenses and visual illusion measured at the Louvre Paris'; Enoch, 'In search of the earliest known lenses (dating back 4500 years)'.

22 In 2021, using deep learning allowed a lens so thin that a camera could be as small as a grain of sand, as described in Tseng et al., 'Neural nano-optics for high-quality thin lens imaging'. In 2022, deep learning was used to skip the lens altogether. See Pan et al., 'Lensless inference camera'.

23 Although contemporary textbooks and histories of the camera obscura commonly repeat its being known to Mozi (without

providing specific references), there is some debate on whether or not the Mohist optical canon was describing a camera obscura. The scholar Nathan Sivin notes that, although he himself believes it was, his collaborator A. C. Graham argued that it only referenced 'the inversion of images in general'. Sivin, 'Review of *The Mozi: A Complete Translation*'. Similarly, Aristotle is frequently noted as having mentioned pinhole images, but usually without reference. It appears that the citation is actually from the pseudo-Aristotelian *Problemata*. See Lindberg, 'The theory of pinhole images from antiquity to the thirteenth century'.

24 St John, 'Australian communication design history'.

25 This point is made at the start of Terry Edgerton's book *The Mirror, the Window, and the Telescope: How Renaissance Linear Perspective Changed Our Vision of the Universe*.

26 The 'invisible gorilla' experiment is a great example of this: if you ask people to watch a video of people playing with a ball and to count how many times players in white shirts pass a ball to each other, during which time a person in a gorilla costume walks on screen and beats its chest, half the people won't have noticed the gorilla. Presumably our eyes *saw* the gorilla, but our brains didn't register it because it wasn't important to our goal. Chabris and Simons, *The Invisible Gorilla and Other Ways Our Intuition Deceives Us*.

27 Edgerton, *The Mirror, the Window, and the Telescope*, pp. 5–6. See also Kemp, *The Science of Art*.

28 Edgerton, *The Mirror, the Window, and the Telescope*, p. 7.

29 Ibid., p. 8.

30 For discussions of some of the different ways perspective can be used in digital media, see, for instance, Tovey, 'Photomaps'; Uricchio, 'The algorithmic turn'.

31 Fried et al., 'Perspective-aware manipulation of portrait photos'.

32 Edgerton, *The Mirror, the Window, and the Telescope*, pp. 169–71.

33 Ibid., p. 159.

34 Galileo, *Sidereus nuncius*, 1610, quoted ibid., p. 161.

35 For a history of data visualisation, see Friendly, 'A brief history of data visualization'. My essay on the epistemology of data visualisations also includes some discussion of early data visualisations: Rettberg, 'Ways of knowing with data visualizations'.

36 Advertisements like these can be easily found in the digitised archives of old photography magazines, which are searchable on Google Books and in national libraries. I found a Kodak ad with the 'You press the button' slogan in the November 1889 edition of *The Photographic Herald and Amateur Sportsman* and the Pentax ad by leafing through the digitised August 1984 edition of *Popular Photography*.

37 I can't find the story in current histories of photography, although some rather disreputable websites tell versions where the mercury came from a broken thermometer rather than an uncovered bowl. See Kittler, *Optical Media*, pp. 129–30; Eder, *History of Photography*, pp. 227–8; von Liebig, 'Induction and deduction', p. 303.

38 Kittler, *Optical Media*, p. 130.

39 Emerling, *Photography: History and Theory*, p. 18.

40 Gu, 'What's in a Name?'

41 Picard, 'Racing Jules Lion'; Gu, 'What's in a name?', p. 121.

42 Yi Gu cites this in his paper discussing the changing names in Chinese given to photography from the 1840s on.

43 Ibid., p. 123.

44 Nwafor, 'Photography: Daguerreotype and the African experience'. See also Sigrid Lien, who discusses nineteenth-century photographs of Saami women, using postcolonialist theories in her analysis: Lien, 'Assimilating the wild and the primitive: Lajla and other Sámi heroines in Norwegian fin-de-siècle photography'.

45 Sontag, *On Photography*, p. 4.

46 Ibid., p. 3.

47 Du Bois, *The Souls of Black Folk*, p. 19.

48 Douglass, quoted in Willis, *Reflections in Black: A History of Black Photographers 1840 to the Present*, p. xvi, and in Bernier, 'A visual call to arms against the "caracature [*sic*] of my own face'.

49 Monteiro, 'Gaming faces'.

50 I have described my experience with Heather Dewey-Hagborg's masks in more detail in my blog, where I include links to explanations of the technology from the company Parabon (see https://jilltxt.net/generating-portraits-from-dna-heather-dewey-hagborgs-becoming-chelsea). See also M'charek, Toom and Jong, 'The trouble with race in forensic identification' for more on how race is reinstated as a category through DNA analysis.

51 Carlson-Berne, *Face of Freedom: How the Photos of Frederick Douglass Celebrated Racial Equality*, p. 7.

52 This report of Muybridge's first attempts at the photographs was written up in the newspaper *Daily Alta California* on 7 April 1873 in a short article titled 'Quick work'. The California Digital Newspaper Collection (https://cdnc.ucr.edu) provides access to a digitized version of the newspaper, where you can read the full story and many other short articles about Muybridge.

53 As with photography, many different inventors developed cinematography during the 1880s and 1890s, combining Muybridge's technique with earlier developments such as the zoetrope and the stroboscope.

54 See Rettberg, *Seeing Ourselves through Technology*, pp. 36–40. for a discussion of the popular YouTube genre of time-lapse selfies.

55 Rodin and Gsell, *Rodin on Art and Artists*, p. 34. This quote is discussed at more length in Virilio, *The Vision Machine*, p. 2.

56 Apple also uses other techniques to verify your face, including standard photography, and for security purposes they do not publicise the full workings of FaceID. The infrared dots can, however, be seen if an infrared camera is used.

57 In 1800 William Herschel presented to the Royal Society of London experiments using thermometers to measure the temperature of sunlight that had been separated into its different colours by a prism. He tried measuring beyond the outside ranges of visible light, finding nothing beyond violet, but hotter temperatures beyond red. As he wrote, the experiments 'prove,

that there are rays coming from the sun . . . invested with a high power of heating bodies, but with none of illuminating objects; and this explains the reason why they have hitherto escaped unnoticed.' Herschel, 'Experiments on the refrangibility of the invisible rays of the sun'.

58 Rogalski, 'History of infrared detectors'.

59 The technical information is from Kodak's information sheet about the film, 'Aerial data: Kodak Aerochrome III infrared film 1443'.

60 A book was published documenting *Incoming* when it was exhibited at the Barbican: Mosse and Agamben, *Incoming*, 2017.

61 Saugmann, Möller and Bellmer, 'Seeing like a surveillance agency?'

62 Rettberg, *Seeing Ourselves through Technology*, pp. 25–7.

63 Shklovsky, 'Art as technique'.

64 Bridle, *Ways of Being: Animals, Plants, Machines: The Search for a Planetary Intelligence*, p. 138.

65 See Powers, *The Overstory*, p. 97. The story is presented as a summary of a science fiction novel read by the character Ritu Mehta. In *Ways of Being*, p. 126, Bridle retells it and compares the aliens' way of seeing the world to the way AI might see it.

Chapter 2 Seeing Differently

1 Thomas Stubblefield devotes a whole chapter in *Drone Art: The Everywhere War as Medium* to the similarities between drones and animals. Our tendency to zoomorphise drones isn't just that we think they are similar to birds or, in the case of ground drones like Alfred, to a turtle: in fact, Stubblefield explains in chapter 4 of his book, the early development of drones drew heavily upon animal–machine prototypes.

2 The artwork is documented in Kronman and Zingerle, 'Suspicious behavior'.

3 See chapter 1, 'Thinking otherwise', in Bridle, *Ways of Being: Animals, Plants, Machines: The Search for a Planetary Intelligence*.

4 Hayles, *Unthought: The Power of the Cognitive Nonconscious*,
   p. 22.

5 Vertov, *Kino-Eye: The Writings of Dziga Vertov*.

6 Ibid., p. 14.

7 Cave, Dihal and Dillon, *AI Narratives: A History of Imaginative
   Thinking about Intelligent Machines*.

8 Vertov, *Kino-Eye*, pp. 14–15.

9 Ibid., p. 16.

10 Ibid., p. 17.

11 The film has been digitised by the Austrian Film Museum and
   can be viewed on their YouTube channel (*Kino-Pravda No. 19*).

12 The Austrian Film Museum lists Anatolii Goldobin as chief
   editor of the film, but as Goldobin was the boss of the film production company Goskino, which produced *Kino-Pravda No. 19*
   (Thompson, 'Government policies and practical necessities in
   the Soviet cinema of the 1920s', p. 26), this was likely a proforma
   listing. Svilova was known to be the editor in the Kinoks collective (see Kaganovsky, 'Film editing as women's work: Ėsfir'
   Shub, Elizaveta Svilova, and the culture of Soviet montage'), and
   the sequence shows her doing her job, presumably filmed by the
   cameraman Mikhail Kaufman at Vertov's direction.

13 Thanks to Professor Ingunn Lunde for discussing the Russian
   with me. See also Howell and Krementsov, *The Art and Science of
   Making the New Man in Early 20th-Century Russia*, p. xi, which
   explains that *chelovek* is gender neutral. While they chose to
   translate *novye chelovek* as 'new man' on account of the English
   use of 'man' in the early twentieth century, other scholars have
   translated it as 'new human'. The *Oxford English Dictionary*
   states in its entry on 'man' that 'Man was considered until the
   20th cent. to include women by implication, though referring
   primarily to males. It is now frequently understood to exclude
   women, and is therefore avoided by many people.'

14 Pearlman and Heftberger, 'Editorial: recognising women's work
   as creative work'.

15 Kaganovsky, 'Film editing as women's work'.

16 For a discussion of the Frankfurt School and other mid-twentieth-century philosophers of technology, see Delanty and Harris, 'Critical theory and the question of technology'.

17 Flusser's *Für eine Philosophie der Fotografie* was first published in 1983. The quotations in this paragraph are from the English translation, *Towards a Philosophy of Photography*, pp. 30–2.

18 Ibid., p. 46.

19 Ibid., p. 48.

20 Marx, *Capital: A Critique of Political Economy*, Vol. I, Bk 1, p. 626.

21 Ibid., p. 606.

22 For an example of an early twenty-first-century optimistic take on how technology would liberate us, see Rheingold, *Smart Mobs: The Next Social Revolution*.

23 Qiu, *Goodbye iSlave*.

24 Gillespie, *Custodians of the Internet: Platforms, Content Moderation, and the Hidden Decisions That Shape Social Media*.

25 Asaro, 'The labor of surveillance and bureaucratized killing'.

26 Marx, *Capital*, p. 532.

27 Flusser, *Towards a Philosophy of Photography*, p. 23.

28 Ibid., p. 24.

29 Livingstone, *Vision and Art*, pp. 12–28.

30 Hayles primarily discusses cybersemiotics in her 2019 article 'Can computers create meanings?'. Biosemiotics was first developed by the Estonian scholar Jakob von Uexküll.

31 A general overview of eye optics can be found in Björn, 'The diversity of eye optics'. An overview of differences in visual acuity can be found in Caves, Brandley and Johnsen, 'Visual acuity and the evolution of signals'. The advantages of compound eyes are discussed in papers describing the development of artificial compound eyes, such as Floreano et al., 'Miniature curved artificial compound eyes', or Kogos et al., 'Plasmonic ommatidia for lens-less compound-eye vision'.

32 Brentari, *Jakob von Uexküll: The Discovery of the Umwelt between Biosemiotics and Theoretical Biology*, p. 79 (emphasis in the

original). Anna Tsing, on the other hand, argues that Uexküll focuses too strongly on the individual organism as self-contained, neglecting the assemblages in which they are always participants and the interspecies symbiosis that is necessary for survival and reproduction for many species. Tsing, *The Mushroom at the End of the World*, p. 156. Hayles makes a similar argument to Tsing in 'Can computers create meanings?'.

33 Brentari, *Jakob von Uexküll*, pp. 85–6.

34 See, for instance, Atkin, 'Peirce's theory of signs'. The example of the tree in autumn is from Hayles, 'Can computers create meanings?', p. 40.

35 John Durham Peters's book *The Marvelous Clouds: Toward a Philosophy of Elemental Media* would seem an exception in its explorations of dolphin communication, but Peters does not use scholarship on biosemiotics.

36 Deregowski, 'Real space and represented space', p. 65.

37 Goncharov and Tiapovkin, 'Cultural and environmental factors in the perception of perspective among indigenous tundra inhabitants'.

38 A study of Yoruba people in the mid-twentieth century found they did not recognise drawings on paper but could easily recognise the same drawings if marked on leather or carved into wood, suggesting that paper, not the drawing itself, was the problem. Other examples suggest that pictures recognised as pictures in some cultures are not recognised in other cultures. Deregowski, 'Real space and represented space', pp. 57–8.

39 See White and Yamashita, '*Boquila trifoliolata* mimics leaves of an artificial plastic host plant'. A Twitter thread offering a list of alterative explanations to the plant vision theory was published by Benjamin Schmidt (@benschmidt741) on 29 March 2022 at https://twitter.com/benschmidt741/status/150881054281893 8888.

40 Hayles, 'Can computers create meanings?', p. 41.

41 Ibid., p. 50.

42 The *MIT Technology Review* discussed the sudden failings of AI in an article on 11 May 2020, noting that human intervention was required to adjust AI models (Heaven, 'Our weird behavior during the pandemic is messing with AI models').

43 Buolamwini and Gebru, 'Gender shades'.

44 Raji and Buolamwini, 'Actionable auditing'.

45 McEwan, *Machines Like Me*, p. 139.

46 Haraway, 'A cyborg manifesto', p. 150.

47 Solberg, '(Always) playing the camera: cyborg vision and embodied surveillance in digital games'.

Chapter 3 Seeing Everything

1 The article was published in the *Wednesday Journal*, a local weekly newspaper, on 22 March 2022 and can be read online at www.oakpark.com/2022/03/22/oak-park-board-divided-on-license-plate-reading-tech/.

2 Pew Research Center, 'Americans' trust in scientists, other groups declines'.

3 Redlining was the practice of refusing to insure mortgages in African American neighbourhoods, which was common from the 1930s on and caused increased segregation and inequity between black and white neighbourhoods. Safiya Noble, in *Algorithms of Oppression*, uses the term 'technological redlining' to describe ways technology differentiates between neighbourhoods in ways that reinforce racial inequities similarly to redlining.

4 As Lasse Hodne writes in 'Omnivoyance and omnipresence: word and vision according to Nicholas of Cusa and Jan van Eyck', this was a technique that was particularly common in Christian art, where it can be interpreted as a demonstration of God's omnivoyance, but the technique was also used in secular images, ranging from an ancient statue of Athena to the Mona Lisa. Max Liljefors, in his chapter 'Omniscience and blindness' in Liljefors, Noll and Steuer, *War and Algorithm*, p. 129, also notes this phenomenon.

5 Ibid., pp. 129–30.

6   Koellner, 'The "all-seeing community"', p. 53, quoting Schmidt-Burkhardt, 'The all-seer: God's eye as proto-surveillance'.

7   De Seta, 'Technologies of clairvoyance: Chinese lineages and mythologies of machine vision'.

8   A popular history of some of these aerial surveillance systems can be found in Michel, *Eyes in the Sky: The Secret Rise of Gorgon Stare and How it Will Watch Us All.*

9   The chapter 'Internet of animals' has fascinating examples of this and a discussion of the Argos system as well as other tracking systems for animals and wildlife. See Bridle, *Ways of Being: Animals, Plants, Machines: The Search for a Planetary Intelligence.*

10 This is from John 20:25 in the King James version of the Bible. Jesus allows Thomas to thrust his finger into the wound in his side, after which Thomas believes that Jesus is truly reborn.

11 See Mayor, *Gods and Robots: Ancient Dreams of Technology*, p. 137. Bentham's idea of the panopticon was famously adopted by Michel Foucault as a metaphor for how discipline became internalised in individuals in the twentieth century through surveillance and the awareness that you might be being watched.

12 Foucault, *Discipline and Punish: The Birth of the Prison.*

13 Andrejevic and Selwyn, *Facial Recognition*, p. 46.

14 Mungwini, '"Surveillance and cultural panopticism"', p. 350.

15 The 'running gun battle' is described in a *Chicago Tribune* article by Deborah Kadin, published on 12 November 2021, titled 'Gunmen in two cars drive through Oak Park shooting at each other; three homes struck'. The video was published on the website *West Cook News* on 10 November 2021 in an article titled 'Watch video of the Sat. Nov. 7 Oak Park shootout' (https://westcooknews.com/stories/612156903-watch-video-of-the-sat-nov-7-oak-park-shootout; it can also be found on YouTube at https://youtu.be/wb4_92xz4oc). It is worth noting that *West Cook News* is a far-right website known for posting controversial and sometimes misleading takes on local news to stir up debate and anger (see, for instance, 'Beware partisan "pink slime" sites that pose as local news', by Margaret Sullivan in the *Washington*

Post of 5 June 2022; www.washingtonpost.com/media/2022/06
/05/pink-slime-west-cook-news-school-race-grading/).

16 Oak Park is governed by an elected board of six trustees and a
president (like a mayor). The village board sets policy and hires a
village manager to oversee the day-to-day operations. Actually,
there are many other boards in Oak Park as well, each levying its
own taxes for its area: the township is in charge of social services
and mental health, and the library, schools and parks all have
their own boards and levy their own taxes. The village board is
in charge of the police force and public infrastructure, so when
the police department asked for Flock cameras, it was the village
board's decision to make.

17 My quotations from and discussions of the village board meetings
are based on the archived videos at the Oak Park website and the
meeting's minutes: Village of Oak Park, 'Meeting minutes, village
board meeting March 21, 2022'.

18 Andrejevic, *Automated Media*, p. 119.

19 Max Liljefors explores the idea of the pointless view in his chapter 'Omnivoyance and Blindness' in Liljefors, Noll and Steuer,
War and Algorithm. The concept is further elaborated by Allen
Feldman in the final chapter of the same book, 'Of the pointless
view: from the ecotechnology to the echotheology of omnivoyant
war'.

20 In 2022, a stationary Flock licence plate reader camera cost
$2,500. A decade earlier, a stationary camera could cost up to
$100,000, and the more common mobile readers owned by many
police districts cost between $10,000 and $25,000. Koper and
Lum, 'The impacts of large-scale license plate reader deployment
on criminal investigations', p. 321.

21 Sarah Brayne's in-depth analysis of how surveillance technologies are used by the police in Los Angeles, based on extensive
fieldwork in LAPD, provides extremely useful background on
this shift. See Brayne, *Predict and Surveil: Data, Discretion, and
the Future of Policing*.

22 Ibid., p. 14.

23 Elizabeth E. Joh, in 'Reckless automation in policing', argues that decentralisation is a reason why invasive technology is so rapidly adapted in US police departments.

24 Rekor markets the Watchman Scout (which used to be called the Watchman Home) as part of its OpenALPR software suite (www .openalpr.com/software/scout). See Simonite, 'AI license plate readers are cheaper – so drive carefully'.

25 Rekor provides 'actionable solutions for intelligent infrastructure', including but not limited to ALPRs. See http://rekor.ai.

26 The video 'Memphis area city commissioner on why his city partners with Flock Safety' shows Wesley Wright, Lakeland Tennessee commissioner, talking about why he is happy with Flock in his community. It is posted on Flock Safety's account on 24 February 2021; https://youtu.be/10S5EnVEAOs.

27 Koellner, 'The "all-seeing community"'.

28 The quote by the pastor is from a video interview and written news story about the fundraising published in Live 5 WCSC News on 3 November 2019 by Lillian Donahue titled 'Charleston East Side community members raising money for surveillance cameras to help curb crime'; www.live5news.com/2019/11/04 /charleston-east-side-community-members-raising-money-sur veillance-cameras-help-curb-crime /.

29 Oak Park is also known for support of LGBTQ+ groups, both as a welcoming neighbourhood and through policy and representation. When Joanne Trapani was elected to the village board in 1997 she was the first open lesbian to be elected to the legislature in Illinois. She became village president in 2001. See the *Wednesday Journal*, 9 December 2020; www.oakpark.com/2020 /12/09/remembering-joanne-trapani/.

30 Streets in Oak Park, as in much of the US, are organised in a very regular grid fashion, and each block has houses numbered in a particular hundred, so everyone knows that the 300 block of North Oak Park Avenue, for instance, is three blocks north of the train tracks downtown.

31 Peterman, 'Our history'.

32 McKenzie, 'The politics of school desegregation in Oak Park, Illinois'.

33 See the report 'Alarming racial disparities in Oak Park policing', prepared by the community group Freedom to Thrive in Oak Park in 2020; www.freedomtothriveop.com/blog/alarming-racial-disparities-in-oak-park-policing.

34 Chicago Metropolitan Agency for Planning, 'Community data snapshots for Austin and Oak Park'.

35 For more on how racism has shaped US society and technology in particular, see Kendi, *Stamped from the Beginning*; Benjamin, *Race after Technology: Abolitionist Tools for the New Jim Code*.

36 See Kurwa, 'Building the digitally gated community'. Kurwa was writing about Nextdoor, a predecessor to Neighbors launched in 2011 that was not affiliated with a smart camera but is otherwise very similar. While Neighbors is (as of 2022) only available in the USA, Nextdoor is also available in several European countries, as well as Canada, Australia and the UK.

37 To protect the privacy of the people on Neighbors, the comments quoted are fabrications that are representative composites of actual comments. This method is taken from Markham, 'Fabrication as ethical practice: qualitative inquiry in ambiguous internet contexts'.

38 The Amalgamated Transit Workers Union Local 308 says they want conductors back, and I agree. 'CTA union leader demands return of conductors and CTA's own police unit to combat crime surge', *Chicago Sun-Times*, 9 March 2022.

39 Rettberg, 'Ways of knowing with data visualizations'.

40 The incident took place on Saturday, 25 March 2022, at about 1:55 am and was reported by many news sources, including ABC Eyewitness News in an article published later that day titled 'CTA employee involved in fight-turned-shooting that critically injured man at Red Line station'.

41 See the news article 'University of Chicago student shot while sitting on Green Line train dies after days in hospital' on *WGN9*

on 5 July 2021; https://wgntv.com/news/chicago-news/univer sity-of-chicago-student-shot-while-sitting-on-green-line-train -dies-after-days-in-hospital/.

42 A video of the encounter was published by NBC News in the story 'Black woman whose family was handcuffed at gunpoint by police sues Aurora, Colorado', by Doha Mandani, 25 January 2021. It can be viewed at www.nbcnews.com/news/nbcblk/black -woman-whose-family-was-handcuffed-gunpoint-aurora-colora do-police-n1255586.

43 The meeting minutes from the 21 March 2022 meeting are available at https://t.co/Av6limyrJj, and a video of the full meeting, which was held on Zoom, can be viewed at https://oak-park.gra nicus.com/player/clip/1815. The village manager's presentation on Flock starts 52 minutes into the video.

44 Benjamin, *Race after Technology*, pp. 44–5.

45 Piza et al., 'CCTV surveillance for crime prevention'.

46 The ShotSpotter website: http://shotspotter.com.

47 The study was conducted by the MacArthur Justice Center in 2021: http://endpolicesurveillance.com.

48 Ferguson and Witzburg, 'The Chicago Police Department's use of Shotspotter technology', p. 3.

49 Ibid., p. 19.

50 A lawsuit was filed against the Chicago police based on this and another wrongful arrest by the MacArthur Justice Center at Northwestern University; it is discussed in an AP News story by journalists Garance Burke and Michael Tarm on 21 July 2022: 'Lawsuit: Chicago police misused ShotSpotter in murder case'; https://apnews.com/article/gun-violence-technology-crime-chi cago-lawsuits-3e6145f63c96593866cf89ac01ce7498.

51 Doucette et al., 'Impact of ShotSpotter technology on firearm homicides and arrests among large metropolitan counties'.

52 Ratcliffe et al., 'A partially randomized field experiment on the effect of an acoustic gunshot detection system on police incident reports'.

53 Ferguson and Witzburg, 'The Chicago Police Department's use of Shotspotter technology', p. 22.

54 Nowicki, 'State police tout 20 arrests, new tech in highway shootings'.

55 The World Values Survey consistently ranks Norway and the other Nordic countries as countries with very high levels of trust, while the USA is around the global average. The website Ourworld indata.org visualises data from the survey, showing that over 70 per cent of Norwegians agreed that 'most people can be trusted', while only around 40 per cent of people in the United States feel the same. Trust in institutions has dropped in the USA since the pandemic. A survey by the Pew Research Center, 'Increasing public criticism, confusion over COVID-19 response in U.S.', found that trust in the CDC (the Centers for Disease Control) dropped from 88 per cent in March 2020 to just 50 per cent in January 2022, while trust in local and state elected officials dropped from 69 per cent and 70 per cent to 50 per cent and 46 per cent respectively.

56 Molina and Sundar, 'Does distrust in humans predict greater trust in AI?'

57 For an overview of research on the connection between exposure to crime news and people's perception of crime being common, and on the increased coverage of crime since the Second World War, see Näsi et al., 'Crime news consumption and fear of violence'. This phenomenon is valid for other types of collectively experienced crisis as well, ranging from terrorist attacks, racial violence, economic precarity and climate change to pandemics. An overview of how individuals' mental and physical health is affected by media exposure after terrorist attacks, epidemics and other societal crises is given in Garfin, Silver and Holman, 'The novel coronavirus (COVID-2019) outbreak'. An additional factor today is that current crises, especially in the USA, are 'chronic events with an ambiguous endpoint'. See Silver, Holman and Garfin, 'Coping with cascading collective traumas in the United States'.

58 Gramlich, 'Voters' perceptions of crime continue to conflict with reality'.

59 Näsi et al., 'Crime news consumption and fear of violence', p. 579.

Chapter 4 Being Seen

1 The 'cooperative gaze hypothesis' holds that the greater visibilty of the whites of our eyes leads to more social cooperation in humans compared to other primates, as argued in Tomasello et al., 'Reliance on head versus eyes in the gaze following of great apes and human infants'. For a popular science account of this and other aspects of humans' social and collaborative nature, see Bregman, *Humankind*, p. 69.

2 Mulvey, 'Visual pleasure and narrative cinema'.

3 Bogost, 'Your phone wasn't built for the apocalypse'.

4 Lum, '"Racist" camera phenomenon explained – almost'.

5 Frosh, *The Poetics of Digital Media*, p. 121.

6 I explore visually the idea that fun biometrics might make us less sceptical of other uses of biometrics in a Snapchat story I made in 2016. For documentation, see Rettberg, 'Snapchat research stories'.

7 This describes the dataset on which the DALL-E image generation model is trained. The developers document the biases, risks and limitations of the model here: https://github.com/openai/dalle-2-preview/blob/main/system-card.md.

8 For a more detailed discussion of how our contemporary understanding of normality came into being, see Cryle and Stephens, *Normality*. They discuss Quetelet's idealisation of the average man on pp 79–81.

9 Davis, 'Introduction: disability, normality, and power', p. 2.

10 Daniels, 'The "average man"?' For a contemporary reading of Daniels's study that relates it to technology, see Wachter-Boettcher, *Technically Wrong*, pp. 27–48.

11 *Zizi – Queering the Dataset* is the first of a series of works in the Zizi project. Documentation of the works can be found at Jake

Elwes's website, https://jakeelwes.com/. Elwes describes the process of creating the queered dataset in a conference presentation that is available on YouTube: Elwes, 'Queering datasets'; www.youtube.com/watch?v=5ukrHDnm6rQ.

12 See Barker, 'Making-up on mobile'.

13 The paper documenting the dataset does not give any details about how the attributes were chosen or how the annotation was done, beyond its being done by 'a professional labeling company'. Liu et al., 'Deep learning face attributes in the wild'.

14 A data paper describing the dataset is available at Rettberg et al., 'Representations of machine vision technologies in artworks, games and narratives: documentation of a dataset'.

15 Gates, *Our Biometric Future: Facial Recognition Technology and the Culture of Surveillance*, p. 8.

16 For an extensive review of psychological scholarship on the relationship between facial expressions and emotions, see Barrett et al., 'Emotional expressions reconsidered'.

17 Goffman, *The Presentation of Self in Everyday Life*.

18 See the article 'Smile for the camera: the dark side of China's emotion recognition tech', *The Guardian*, 3 March 2021; www.theguardian.com/global-development/2021/mar/03/china-positive-energy-emotion-surveillance-recognition-tech. A story by Xue Yujie in the newsletter *Sixth Tone* describes emotion recognition in schools in China: 'Camera above the classroom', 26 March 2019; www.sixthtone.com/news/1003759/camera-above-the-classroom.

19 Pierce, 'Smart home security cameras and shifting lines of creepiness'.

20 Barker, 'Making-up on mobile'; Lavrence and Cambre, '"Do I look like my selfie?'

21 The blog post about the Tansøy store, written by Lisa Myklebust on 23 June 2022, is available at www.mat-norge.no/blog/nærbutikken-tansøy-er-blitt-digitalisert-bra-for-kunden-og-bra-for-butikken. Mat-Norge's first unstaffed shop was Hegna landhandel in Seljord, which went unstaffed on 16 November 2019. The

video on their website frames the opening in intense national romanticism: a Hardanger fiddle plays a winsome tune as the camera zooms in on the shop, which is located in a rebuilt red barn. The mayor holds a speech, dressed in her national costume and with Norwegian flags: https://hegnalandhandel.no.

22 For businesses that are interested in using the system in their shops, Amazon explains how the Just Walk Out technology works on their website: https://justwalkout.com/faq.

23 Bentalha and Hmioui, 'Smart service supply chain and Just Walk Out technology'.

24 McCosker and Wilken, *Automating Vision: The Social Implications of the New Camera Consciousness*.

25 See issue 3/2018 of *Bibliotekaren* for a series of articles about unstaffed libraries in Norway: www.bibforb.no/bibliotekaren.

26 See, for instance, Claire Zulkey, 'Give them shelter?', in *American Libraries*, 3 June 2019; https://americanlibrariesmagazine.org/20 19/06/03/give-them-shelter-library-camping-bans/.

27 I translated the quote from Svardahl from a Norwegian-language story published by Mat-Norge, the company that has developed the system, on 23 June 2022: 'Nærbutikken Tansøy er blitt digitalisert: – bra for kunden, og bra for butikken!'; www.mat-nor ge.no/blog/nærbutikken-tansøy-er-blitt-digitalisert-bra-for-kun den-og-bra-for-butikken. In Sweden, rather than digitising existing small shops, the company Lifvs is setting up standardised containers in rural areas lacking grocery stores. These contain miniature self-service grocery shops where customers use an app to enter, to scan each item they take, and to check out. See https://lifvs.com.

28 News story in *Avisa Sør-Trøndelag*, 20 December 2021: 'Mistenker tyveri av egg fra ubemannet butikk'; www.avisa-st.no /nyheter/i/y4KmLa/mistenker-tyveri-av-egg-fra-ubemannet-bu tikk.

29 See Claire Zulkey, 'Automatic for the people', in *American Libraries*, 3 September 2019; https://americanlibrariesmagazine .org/2019/09/03/automatic-people-self-service-libraries/.

30 Selwyn, Campbell and Andrejevic, 'Autoroll'. Script analysis was introduced by the French sociologist of technology Madeleine Akrich, one of the scholars who developed actor-network theory with Bruno Latour and others, in her 1992 article 'The de-scription of technical objects'.

31 The quote is from a BBC article about the case, 'Schools pause facial recognition lunch plans', 25 October 2021; www.bbc.com /news/technology-59037346.

32 Akrich, 'The de-scription of technical objects', pp. 208–9.

33 Goffman gives the example of earlier generations' hat-tipping, which is done 'to show regard while simultaneously restoring the doer and recipient to a state of mutual civil inattention' (Goffman, *Relations in Public: Microstudies of the Public Order*, p. 92). Today we would show civil inattention by a quick nod, or simply making space for each other when we pass on a sidewalk.

34 Bigby and Wiesel, 'Using the concept of encounter to further the social inclusion of people with intellectual disabilities'.

35 Brautigan printed copies of the poem and passed them out for free on the streets of San Francisco. It is widely available online, including at http://allpoetry.com.

36 Bridle, *Ways of Being: Animals, Plants, Machines: The Search for a Planetary Intelligence*.

37 Shusterman, *Thunderhead*, p. 59.

38 Ibid., p. 157.

39 I discuss some of these in *Seeing Ourselves through Technology*, pp. 65–8.

40 For a fascinating discussion of how coming-of-age novels for young adults deal with technology in ways that closely align with posthumanist theory, see Flanagan, *Technology and Identity in Young Adult Fiction: The Posthuman Subject*.

41 The Norwegian Center for Holocaust and Minority Studies has a website with extensive information about the Holocaust in Norway at www.hlsenteret.no. I am using their numbers, from a page on their website titled 'Deportasjonen av de norske jødene'. For a comprehensive history of Jewish people in

Norway, see Mendelsohn, *Jødenes Historie i Norge Gjennom 300 År*. Mendelsohn also published an English-language article in 1981 with slightly different numbers: 'Actions against the Jews in Norway during the war'.

42 My translation from German. The original read *Die augenblichlichen Zeitverhältnisse erfordern dringend eine genaue Überwachung der personenverkehrs in Norwegen*, and is quoted in Søbye, 'Et mørkt kapittel i statistikkens historie?', p. 9, an article with a thorough discussion of the role of the National Bureau of Statistics during the Holocaust. Synne Corell provides a detailed history of the persecution and murder of Jews in Norway in her 2021 book *Likvidasjonen: historien om holocaust i Norge og jakten på jødenes eiendom*. See also Seltzer and Anderson, 'The dark side of numbers: the role of population data systems in human rights abuses'.

43 Shusterman, *Thunderhead*, p. 75.

Chapter 5 Seeing Less

1 The 'emotion picture' of *Dirty Computer* is a narrative music video that tells a cohesive story for the whole album about a near-future, homophobic, totalitarian society trying to erase Janelle's memories and recast her as 'Jane 57821'.

2 See Ragnhild Solberg's paper '(Always) playing the camera' for an analysis of how the player interactions with surveillance cameras in *Watch Dogs: Legion* and *Final Fantasy VII* draw attention to an embodied experience of machine vision that Solberg calls cyborg vision. Linda Kronman discusses similar themes in digital artworks in the paper 'Hacking machine vision'.

3 Mills, 'Afghano-Persian trickster women: definitions, liminalities, and gender', p. 33.

4 Najmabadi, 'Reading – and enjoying – "wiles of women" stories as a feminist', p. 214.

5 Ytre-Arne and Moe, 'Folk theories of algorithms'.

6 Bishop, 'Algorithmic experts'.

7 Van der Nagel, '"Networks that work too well"'.

8 Gerrard, 'Beyond the hashtag'.

9 Szegedy et al., 'Intriguing properties of neural networks'.

10 This point was made by Google Brain Research engineer Nicholas Frosst in a keynote speech at the ReWork Deep Learning Summit in Montreal in 2019. It was reported in *Synced: AI Technology & Industry Review* on 21 November 2019; https://syncedreview .com/2019/11/21/google-brains-nicholas-frosst-on-adversarial -examples-and-emotional-responses/.

11 Harvey, *CV Dazzle*.

12 This was reported on by the Australian ABC News in a story titled 'Hong Kong protesters cut down data-collecting lamppost', 24 August 2019; www.abc.net.au/news/2019-08-24/hong-kong -protests-smart-lampposts-cut-down-surveillance-fears/1144 5606.

13 Andrejevic and Selwyn, *Facial Recognition*, p. 126.

14 Buolamwini, 'How I'm fighting bias in algorithms'.

15 Buolamwini and Gebru, 'Gender shades'.

16 See, for instance, the cases of Robert Williams, Michael Oliver and Nijeer Parks. A summary is available in an article in *Wired* by Khari Johnson, 7 March 2022: www.wired.com/story/wrong ful-arrests-ai-derailed-3-mens-lives/.

17 Andrejevic and Selwyn, *Facial Recognition*, pp. 97, 112.

18 Browne, *Dark Matters*, p. 26.

19 The artists describe *Mask.ID* on their website, at https://pen.gg /campaign/mask-id-2. The work was exhibited in the Affenfaust Galerie in Hamburg in 2018 (https://affenfaustgalerie.de/en/sh ow/peng-maskid).

Conclusion

1 Buolamwini and Gebru, 'Gender shades'. A number of influential books address the issue of algorithmic bias. See, for instance, Chun, *Discriminating Data: Correlation, Neighborhoods, and the New Politics of Recognition*; Benjamin, *Race after Technology: Abolitionist Tools for the New Jim Code*; Eubanks, *Automating Inequality*; and Noble, *Algorithms of Oppression*.

2 Bennett, *Influx and Efflux*. See also the Institute for Precarious
   Consciousness's 'We are all very anxious: six theses on anxiety
   and why it is effectively preventing militancy, and one possible
   strategy for overcoming it'.

References

Akrich, Madeleine, 'The de-scription of technical objects', in *Shaping Technology/Building Society: Studies in Sociotechnical Change*, ed. Wiebe E. Bijker and John Law. Cambridge, MA: MIT Press, 1992, pp. 205–24.

Andrejevic, Mark, *Automated Media*. London: Routledge, 2019.

Andrejevic, Mark, and Neil Selwyn, *Facial Recognition*. Cambridge: Polity, 2022.

Asaro, Peter M., 'The labor of surveillance and bureaucratized killing: new subjectivities of military drone operators', *Social Semiotics* 23/2 (2013): 196–224; https://doi.org/10.1080/10350330.2013.777591.

Atkin, Albert, 'Peirce's theory of signs', in *The Stanford Encyclopedia of Philosophy*, ed. Edward N. Zalta. Summer 2013 edn; https://plato.stanford.edu/archives/sum2013/entries/peirce-semiotics.

Barker, Jessica, 'Making-up on mobile: the pretty filters and ugly implications of Snapchat', *Fashion, Style & Popular Culture* 7/2 (2020): 207–21; https://doi.org/10.1386/fspc_00015_1.

Barrett, Lisa Feldman, Ralph Adolphs, Stacy Marsella, Aleix M. Martinez and Seth D. Pollak, 'Emotional expressions reconsidered:

challenges to inferring emotion from human facial movements', *Psychological Science in the Public Interest* 20/1 (2019): 1–68; https://doi.org/10.1177/1529100619832930.

Baudry, Jean-Louis, 'Ideological effects of the basic cinematographic apparatus', in *Narrative, Apparatus, Ideology: A Film Theory Reader*, ed. Philip Rosen. New York: Columbia University Press, 1986, pp. 286–98.

Bekhta, Natalya, 'We-narratives: the distinctiveness of collective narration', *Narrative* 25/2 (2017): 164–81; https://doi.org/10.1353/nar.2017.0008.

Benjamin, Ruha, *Race after Technology: Abolitionist Tools for the New Jim Code*. Cambridge: Polity, 2019.

Bennett, Jane, *Vibrant Matter: A Political Economy of Things*. Durham, NC: Duke University Press, 2010.

———. *Influx and Efflux: Writing Up with Walt Whitman*. Durham, NC: Duke University Press, 2020.

Bentalha, Badr, and Aziz Hmioui, 'Smart service supply chain and Just Walk Out technology: a netnographic approach', in *Innovations in Smart Cities Applications*, Vol. 5, ed. Mohamed Ben Ahmed, Anouar Abdelhakim Boudhir, İsmail Rakıp Karaş, Vipul Jain and Sehl Mellouli. Cham: Springer International, 2022, pp. 223–36; https://doi.org/10.1007/978-3-030-94191-8_18.

Bernier, Celeste-Marie, 'A visual call to arms against the "caracature [*sic*] of my own face": from fugitive slave to fugitive image in Frederick Douglass's theory of portraiture', *Journal of American Studies* 49/2 (2015): 323–57; https://doi.org/10.1017/S0021875815000109.

Bigby, Christine, and Ilan Wiesel, 'Using the concept of encounter to further the social inclusion of people with intellectual disabilities: what has been learned?', *Research and Practice in Intellectual and Developmental Disabilities* 6/1 (2019): 39–51; https://doi.org/10.1080/23297018.2018.1528174.

Bishop, Sophie, 'Algorithmic experts: selling algorithmic lore on YouTube', *Social Media + Society* 6/1 (2020); https://doi.org/10.1177/2056305119897323.

Björn, Lars Olaf, 'The diversity of eye optics', in *Photobiology: The Science of Light and Life*, ed. Lars Olaf Björn. 3rd edn, New York: Springer, 2015.

Bogost, Ian, 'Your phone wasn't built for the apocalypse', *The Atlantic*, 11 September 2020; www.theatlantic.com/technology/archive/20 20/09/camera-phone-wildfire-sky/616279/.

Bohigian, George M., 'An ancient eye test – using the stars', *Survey of Ophthalmology* 53/5 (2008): 536–9; https://doi.org/10.1016/j.sur vophthal.2008.06.009.

Bommasani, Rishi, Drew A. Hudson, Ehsan Adeli, et al., 'On the opportunities and risks of foundation models', *arXiv*, 2021; https://doi.org/10.48550/ARXIV.2108.07258.

Braidotti, Rosi, 'A theoretical framework for the critical posthumanities', *Theory, Culture & Society* 36/6 (2019): 31–61; https://doi.org/10.1177/0263276418771486.

Brayne, Sarah, *Predict and Surveil: Data, Discretion, and the Future of Policing*. New York: Oxford University Press, 2021.

Bregman, Rutger, *Humankind: A Hopeful History*, trans. Elizabeth Manton and Erica Moore. London: Bloomsbury, 2020.

Brentari, Carlo, *Jakob von Uexküll: The Discovery of the Umwelt between Biosemiotics and Theoretical Biology*. Dordrecht: Springer, 2015.

Bridle, James, *Ways of Being: Animals, Plants, Machines: The Search for a Planetary Intelligence*. New York: Farrar, Straus & Giroux, 2022.

Brown, Tom B., Benjamin Mann, Nick Ryder, et al., 'Language models are few-shot learners', *arXiv*, 2020; http://arxiv.org/abs/2005.14165.

Browne, Simone, *Dark Matters: On the Surveillance of Blackness*. Durham, NC: Duke University Press, 2015.

Buolamwini, Joy, 'How I'm fighting bias in algorithms', November 2016; www.ted.com/talks/joy_buolamwini_how_i_m_fighting_bi as_in_algorithms.

Buolamwini, Joy, and Timnit Gebru, 'Gender shades: intersectional accuracy disparities in commercial gender classification',

Proceedings of Machine Learning Research 81 (2018): 77–91; http://proceedings.mlr.press/v81/buolamwini18a.html.

Carlson-Berne, Emma, *Face of Freedom: How the Photos of Frederick Douglass Celebrated Racial Equality*. North Mankato, MN: Compass Point Books, 2018.

Cave, Stephen, Kanta Dihal and Sarah Dillon, eds, *AI Narratives: A History of Imaginative Thinking about Intelligent Machines*. Oxford: Oxford University Press, 2020.

Caves, Eleanor M., Nicholas C. Brandley and Sönke Johnsen, 'Visual acuity and the evolution of signals', *Trends in Ecology & Evolution* 33/5 (2018): 358–72; https://doi.org/10.1016/j.tree.2018.03.001.

Chabris, Christopher F., and Daniel Simons, *The Invisible Gorilla and Other Ways Our Intuition Deceives Us*. London: Harper, 2011.

Chicago Metropolitan Agency for Planning, 'Community data snapshots for Austin and Oak Park', August 2021; www.cmap.illino is.gov/data/community-snapshots#Community_Data_Snapshot _map_2017.

Chun, Wendy Hui Kyong, *Discriminating Data: Correlation, Neighborhoods, and the New Politics of Recognition*. Cambridge, MA: MIT Press, 2022.

Conley, Tom, 'Apparatus theory, plain and simple', in *The Anthem Handbook of Screen Theory*, ed. Hunter Vaughan and Tom Conley. London: Anthem Press, 2018, pp. 145–56.

Corell, Synne, *Likvidasjonen: historien om holocaust i Norge og jakten på jødenes eiendom*. Oslo: Gyldendal, 2021.

Crawford, Kate, *Atlas of AI: Power, Politics, and the Planetary Costs of Artificial Intelligence*. New Haven, CT: Yale University Press, 2021.

Crawford, Kate, and Trevor Paglen, *Excavating AI: The Politics of Images in Machine Learning Training Sets*, 19 September 2019. www.excavating.ai.

Cryle, P. M., and Elizabeth Stephens, *Normality: A Critical Genealogy*. Chicago: University of Chicago Press, 2017.

Daniels, Gilbert S., 'The "average man"?', technical note. Yellow Springs, OH: Air Force Aerospace Medical Research Lab, Wright

Air Development Center, December 1952; https://apps.dtic.mil/sti/citations/AD0010203.

Davis, Lennard J., 'Introduction: disability, normality, and power', in *The Disability Studies Reader*, ed. Lennard J. Davis. Florence, KY: Taylor & Francis, 2013, pp. 1–17.

de Seta, Gabriele, 'APAIC report on the holocode crisis', *Surveillance & Society* 19/4 (2021): 474–9; https://doi.org/10.24908/ss.v19i4.15154.

———. '*Huanlian*, or changing faces: deepfakes on Chinese digital media platforms', *Convergence: The International Journal of Research into New Media Technologies* 27/4 (2021): 935–53; https://doi.org/10.1177/13548565211030185.

———. 'Technologies of clairvoyance: Chinese lineages and mythologies of machine vision', in *Machine Decision Is Not Final: China and the History and Future of AI*, ed. Benjamin Bratton, Anna Greenspan and Bogna Konior. Cambridge, MA: MIT Press, 2023.

DeLanda, Manuel, *Assemblage Theory*. Edinburgh: Edinburgh University Press, 2016.

Delanty, Gerard, and Neal Harris, 'Critical theory and the question of technology: the Frankfurt School revisited', *Thesis Eleven* 166/1 (2021): 88–108; https://doi.org/10.1177/07255136211002055.

Deleuze, Gilles, and Félix Guattari, *A Thousand Plateaus: Capitalism and Schizophrenia*. London: Athlone Press, 1988.

Deregowski, J. B., 'Real space and represented space: cross-cultural perspectives', *Behavioral and Brain Sciences* 12/1 (1989): 51–74; https://doi.org/10.1017/S0140525X00024286.

Dijck, José van, 'Datafication, dataism and dataveillance: big data between scientific paradigm and ideology', *Surveillance & Society* 12/2 (2014): 197–208.

Doucette, Mitchell L., Christa Green, Jennifer Necci Dineen, David Shapiro and Kerri M. Raissian, 'Impact of ShotSpotter technology on firearm homicides and arrests among large metropolitan counties: a longitudinal analysis, 1999–2016', *Journal of Urban Health* 98/5 (2021): 609–21; https://doi.org/10.1007/s11524-021-00515-4.

Du Bois, W. E. B., *The Souls of Black Folk: Essays and Sketches*. Durham, NC: Duke Classics, 2012; www.overdrive.com/search?q= D42445D0-B8A5-4350-964B-F8AD8AA978D4.

Eder, Joseph Maria, *History of Photography*, trans. Edward Epstean. New York: Dover, 1945.

Edgerton, Samuel Y., *The Mirror, the Window, and the Telescope: How Renaissance Linear Perspective Changed Our Vision of the Universe*. Ithaca, NY: Cornell University Press, 2009.

Elwes, Jake, 'Queering datasets', 2021; https://youtu.be/5ukrHDn m6rQ.

Emerling, Jae, *Photography: History and Theory*. London: Routledge, 2012.

Enoch, J. M., 'Archeological optics: the very first known mirrors and lenses', *Journal of Modern Optics* 54/9 (2007): 1221–39; https:// doi.org/10.1080/09500340600855106.

———. 'In search of the earliest known lenses (dating back 4500 years)', in *Optics and Lasers in Biomedicine and Culture*, ed. Costas Fotakis, Theodore G. Papazoglou and Costas Kalpouzos. Berlin: Springer, 2000, pp. 3–13; https://doi.org/10.1007/978-3-6 42-56965-4_1.

Enoch, J., R. Heitz, P. Rigault, et al., 'Lenses and visual illusion measured at the Louvre Paris: the eyes of the statue 'Le scribe accroupi', 2018; https://doi.org/10.13140/RG.2.2.24556.67209.

Eubanks, Virginia, *Automating Inequality: How High-Tech Tools Profile, Police, and Punish the Poor*. New York: Picador, 2017.

Ferguson, Joseph M., and Deborah Witzburg, 'The Chicago Police Department's use of Shotspotter technology', 21 August 2021.

Flanagan, Victoria, *Technology and Identity in Young Adult Fiction: The Posthuman Subject*. Basingstoke: Palgrave Macmillan, 2014.

Floreano, Dario, Ramon Pericet-Camara, Stéphane Viollet, et al., 'Miniature curved artificial compound eyes', *Proceedings of the National Academy of Sciences* 110/23 (2013): 9267–72; https://doi .org/10.1073/pnas.1219068110.

Fludernik, Monika, 'Let us tell you our story: we-narration and its pronominal peculiarities', in *Pronouns in Literature*. London:

Palgrave Macmillan, 2018, pp. 171–92; https://doi.org/10.1057
/978-1-349-95317-2_10.

Flusser, Vilém, *Towards a Philosophy of Photography*. London:
Reaktion Books, 2000.

———.*Into the Universe of Technical Images*. Minneapolis: University
of Minnesota Press, 2011.

Foucault, Michel, *Discipline and Punishment: The Birth of the Prison*.
London: Allen Lane, 1977.

Fried, Ohad, Eli Shechtman, Dan B. Goldman and Adam Finkelstein,
'Perspective-aware manipulation of portrait photos', ACM
Transactions on Graphics (2016); https://research.google.com/pu
bs/pub45481.html.

Friedberg, Anne, *The Virtual Window: From Alberti to Microsoft*.
Cambridge, MA: MIT Press, 2009.

Friendly, Michael, 'A brief history of data visualization', in *Handbook
of Data Visualization*, ed. Chun-houh Chen, Wolfgang Härdle and
Antony Unwin. Berlin: Springer, 2006, pp. 15–56; https://doi.org
/10.1007/978-3-540-33037-0_2.

Frosh, Paul, *The Poetics of Digital Media*. Cambridge: Polity,
2019.

Garfin, Dana Rose, Roxane Cohen Silver and E. Alison Holman,
'The novel coronavirus (COVID-2019) outbreak: amplification of
public health consequences by media exposure', *Health Psychology*
39/5 (2020): 355–7; https://doi.org/10.1037/hea0000875.

Gates, Kelly, *Our Biometric Future: Facial Recognition Technology
and the Culture of Surveillance*. New York: New York University
Press, 2011.

Gerrard, Ysabel, 'Beyond the hashtag: circumventing content moderation on social media', *New Media & Society* 20/12 (2018):
4492–511; https://doi.org/10.1177/1461444818776611.

Gillespie, Tarleton, *Custodians of the Internet: Platforms, Content
Moderation, and the Hidden Decisions That Shape Social Media*.
New Haven, CT: Yale University Press, 2018.

Goffman, Erving, *The Presentation of Self in Everyday Life*. New York:
Anchor Books, 1959.

———. *Relations in Public: Microstudies of the Public Order.* New York: Basic Books, 1971.

Goh, Gabriel, Nick Cammarata, Chelsea Voss, Shan Carter, Michael Petrov, Ludwig Schubert, Alec Radford and Chris Olah, 'Multimodal neurons in artificial neural networks', *Distill* (2021); https://doi.org/10.23915/distill.00030.

Goncharov, O. A., and I. N. Tiapovkin, 'Cultural and environmental factors in the perception of perspective among indigenous tundra inhabitants', *Journal of Russian & East European Psychology* 50/5 (2012): 65–86; https://doi.org/10.2753/RPO1061-040550 0504.

Gramlich, John, 'Voters' perceptions of crime continue to conflict with reality', *Pew Research Center*, 16 November 2016; www.pew research.org/fact-tank/2016/11/16/voters-perceptions-of-crime -continue-to-conflict-with-reality/.

Gu, Yi, 'What's in a name? Photography and the reinvention of visual truth in China, 1840–1911', *Art Bulletin* 95/1 (2013): 120–38; https://doi.org/10.1080/00043079.2013.10786109.

Gunderson, Marianne, 'Populærkulturelle forestillinger av utvidet virkelighet: makt og (u)leselige identiteter når verden blir en skjerm' [Visions of augmented reality in popular culture: power and (un)readable identities when the world becomes a screen], *Tidsskrift for Kjønnsforskning* 45/02–03 (2021): 89–104; https:// doi.org/10.18261/issn.1891-1781-2021-02-03-03.

Gunderson, Marianne, Wester Coenraads, Marc Tuters, Gaurish Thakkar, Diego Alves and Hana Marčetić, 'Machine vision creepy-pasta: surveillance devices in digital horror', Report for Digital Methods Summer School 2020; https://docs.google.com/docu ment/d/1qnALNhjryyFmlU6pPWRRmoZxP2G7yyozfUlRKiYJ rR8/.

Haraway, Donna, 'Situated knowledges: the science question in feminism and the privilege of partial perspective', *Feminist Studies* 14/3 (1988): 575–99.

———. 'A cyborg manifesto: science, technology, and socialist-feminism in the late twentieth century', in *Simians, Cyborgs and*

Women: The Reinvention of Nature. New York: Routledge, 1991, pp. 149–81.

Harvey, Adam, *CV Dazzle*, 2010; https://ahprojects.com/cvdazzle/.

Hayles, N. Katherine, 'Can computers create meanings? A cyber/bio/semiotic perspective', *Critical Inquiry* 46/1 (2019): 32–55; https://doi.org/10.1086/705303.

——. 'Cognitive assemblages: technical agency and human interactions', *Critical Inquiry* 43/1 (2016); https://doi.org/10.1086/688293.

——. *Unthought: The Power of the Cognitive Nonconscious*. Chicago: University of Chicago Press, 2017.

Heaven, Will Douglas, 'Our weird behavior during the pandemic is messing with AI models', *MIT Technology Review*, 11 May 2020; www.technologyreview.com/2020/05/11/1001563/covid-pandemic-broken-ai-machine-learning-amazon-retail-fraud-humans-in-the-loop/.

Herschel, William, 'Experiments on the refrangibility of the invisible rays of the sun', *Philosophical Transactions of the Royal Society of London* 90 (1800): 284–92.

Hildebrand, Julia M., *Aerial Play: Drone Medium, Mobility, Communication, and Culture*. Singapore: Palgrave Macmillan, 2021.

Hodne, Lasse, 'Omnivoyance and omnipresence: word and vision according to Nicholas of Cusa and Jan van Eyck', *Journal of Iconographic Studies* 6 (2013): 237–46; https://doi.org/10.1484/J.IKON.5.102952.

Hoel, Aud Sissel, 'Operative images: inroads to a new paradigm of media theory', in *Image – Action – Space: Situating the Screen in Visual Practice*, ed. Luisa Feiersinger, Kathrin Friedrich and Moritz Queisner. Berlin: De Gruyter, 2018, pp. 11–28; www.degruyter.com/view/books/9783110464979/9783110464979-002/9783110464979-002.xml.

Howell, Yvonne, and Nikolai Krementsov, eds, *The Art and Science of Making the New Man in Early 20th-Century Russia*. London: Bloomsbury Academic, 2021.

Institute for Precarious Consciousness, 'We are all very anxious: six theses on anxiety and why it is effectively preventing militancy, and one possible strategy for overcoming it', *Plan C*, 2014; www.weareplanc.org/blog/we-are-all-very-anxious/.

Joh, Elizabeth E., 'Reckless automation in policing', *Berkeley Technology Law Journal Online* (2022); http://dx.doi.org/10.2139/ssrn.4009911.

Kaganovsky, Lilya, 'Film editing as women's work: Ėsfir' Shub, Elizaveta Svilova, and the culture of Soviet montage', *Apparatus: Film, Media and Digital Cultures in Central and Eastern Europe* no. 6 (2008); www.apparatusjournal.net/index.php/apparatus/article/view/114/303.

Kane, Carolyn L., *Chromatic Algorithms: Synthetic Color, Computer Art, and Aesthetics after Code*. Chicago: University of Chicago Press, 2014.

Kemp, Martin, *The Science of Art: Optical Themes in Western Art from Brunelleschi to Seurat*. New Haven, CT: Yale University Press, 1990.

Kendi, Ibram X., *Stamped from the Beginning: The Definitive History of Racist Ideas in America*. New York: Nation Books, 2016.

Kittler, Friedrich A., *Optical Media: Berlin Lectures 1999*, trans. Anthony Enns. Cambridge: Polity, 2010.

Koellner, Sarah, 'The "all-seeing community": Charleston's Eastside, video surveillance, and the listening task', *Surveillance & Society* 20/1 (2022): 47–63; https://doi.org/10.24908/ss.v20i1.14266.

Kogos, Leonard C., Yunzhe Li, Jianing Liu, Yuyu Li, Lei Tian and Roberto Paiella, 'Plasmonic ommatidia for lensless compound-eye vision', *Nature Communications* 11/1 (2020): 1637; https://doi.org/10.1038/s41467-020-15460-0.

Koper, Christopher S., and Cynthia Lum, 'The impacts of large-scale license plate reader deployment on criminal investigations', *Police Quarterly* 22/3 (2019): 305–29; https://doi.org/10.1177/1098611119828039.

Kronman, Linda, 'Classifying humans: the indirect reverse operativity of machine vision', *Photographies*, forthcoming 2023.

——. 'The deception of an infinite view: exploring machine vision in digital art', *Proceedings of POM Beirut 2019*, pp. 70–7; https://dx.doi.org/10.14236/ewic/POM19.11.

——. 'Hacking machine vision', forthcoming.

——. 'Intuition machines: cognizers in complex human-technical assemblages', *APRJA* 9/1 (2020); https://aprja.net/article/view/12 1489.

Kronman, Linda, and Andreas Zingerle, 'Suspicious behavior: a fictional annotation tutorial', in *Nordic Human–Computer Interaction Conference*. Aarhus, Denmark: ACM, 2022; https://doi.org/10.1145/3546155.3547288.

Kurgan, Laura, *Close Up at a Distance: Mapping, Technology, and Politics*. Brooklyn, NY: Zone Books, 2013; https://doi.org/10.2307/j.ctt14bs159.

Kurwa, Rahim, 'Building the digitally gated community: the case of Nextdoor', *Surveillance & Society* 17/1–2 (2019): 111–17; https://doi.org/10.24908/ss.v17i1/2.12927.

Lavrence, Christine, and Carolina Cambre, '"Do I look like my selfie?": Filters and the digital-forensic gaze', *Social Media + Society* 6/4 (2020); https://doi.org/10.1177/2056305120955182.

Lee-Morrison, Lila, *Portraits of Automated Facial Recognition: On Machinic Ways of Seeing the Face*. Bielefeld: Transcript, 2019.

Liebig, Justus von, 'Induction and deduction', *Cornhill Magazine* 12/69 (1965): 296–305.

Lien, Sigrid, 'Assimilating the wild and the primitive: Lajla and other Sámi heroines in Norwegian fin-de-siècle photography', in *Disturbing Pasts: Memories, Controversies and Creativity*, ed. Leon Wainwright. Manchester: Manchester University Press, 2018, pp. 208–24.

Liljefors, Max, Gregor Noll and Daniel Steuer, *War and Algorithm*. London: Rowman & Littlefield, 2019.

Lindberg, David C., 'The theory of pinhole images from antiquity to the thirteenth century', *Archive for History of Exact Sciences* 5/2 (1968); www.jstor.org/stable/41133285.

Liu, Ziwei, Ping Luo, Xiaogang Wang and Xiaoou Tang, 'Deep learning face attributes in the wild', in *Proceedings of IEEE International Conference on Computer Vision (ICCV)*, 2015, pp. 3730–8; www .computer.org/csdl/proceedings-article/iccv/2015/8391d730/12O mNzGlRCR.

Livingstone, Margaret S., *Vision and Art: The Biology of Seeing.* Updated and expanded edn, New York: Abrams, 2013.

Lum, Jessica, '"Racist" camera phenomenon explained – almost', *PetaPixel*, 22 January 2010 [blog]; https://petapixel.com/2010/01 /22/racist-camera-phenomenon-explained-almost/.

McCosker, Anthony, and Rowan Wilken, *Automating Vision: The Social Implications of the New Camera Consciousness.* Abingdon: Routledge, 2020.

McCoy, John P., and Tomer D. Ullman, 'A minimal Turing test', *Journal of Experimental Social Psychology* 79 (2018); https://doi .org/10.1016/j.jesp.2018.05.007.

McEwan, Ian, *Machines Like Me.* London: Random House, 2019.

M'charek, Amade, Victor Toom and Lisette Jong, 'The trouble with race in forensic identification', *Science, Technology, & Human Values* (2020); https://doi.org/10.1177/0162243919899467.

MacKenzie, Donald, and Judy Wajcman, eds, *The Social Shaping of Technology.* Buckingham: Open University Press, 1999.

McKenzie, Evan, 'The politics of school desegregation in Oak Park, Illinois', working paper, Chicago: Great Cities Institute, May 2000.

McLuhan, Marshall, *Understanding Media: The Extensions of Man.* New York: McGraw-Hill, 1964.

Markham, Annette, 'Fabrication as ethical practice: qualitative inquiry in ambiguous internet contexts', *Information, Communication & Society* 15/3 (2012): 334–53; https://doi.org/10.1080/1369118X.20 11.641993.

Marx, Karl, *Capital: A Critique of Political Economy*, Vol. I, Bk 1. London: Electric Book Co., 2001.

Mayor, Adrienne, *Gods and Robots: Ancient Dreams of Technology.* Princeton, NJ: Princeton University Press, 2018.

Meikle, Graham, *Deepfakes.* Cambridge: Polity, 2023.

Mendelsohn, Oskar, 'Actions against the Jews in Norway during the war', *Nordisk Judaistik/Scandinavian Jewish Studies* 3/2 (1981): 27–35; https://doi.org/10.30752/nj.69365.

———. *Jødenes Historie i Norge Gjennom 300 År*, Vol. 2. Oslo: Universitetsforlaget, 1987.

Michel, Arthur Holland, *Eyes in the Sky: The Secret Rise of Gorgon Stare and How it Will Watch Us All*. Boston: Houghton Mifflin Harcourt, 2019.

Mills, Margaret A., 'Afghano-Persian trickster women: definitions, liminalities, and gender', *Marvels & Tales* 32/1 (2018): 33–58; https://doi.org/10.13110/marvelstales.32.1.0033.

Mitchell, Melanie, *Artificial Intelligence: A Guide for Thinking Humans*. New York: Picador, 2020.

Molina, Maria D., and S. Shyam Sundar, 'Does distrust in humans predict greater trust in AI? Role of individual differences in user responses to content moderation', *New Media & Society*, 23 June 2022; https://doi.org/10.1177/14614448221103534.

Monteiro, Stephen, 'Gaming faces: diagnostic scanning in social media and the legacy of racist face analysis', *Information, Communication & Society* (2022); https://doi.org/10.1080/13691 18X.2021.2020867.

Mosse, Richard, and Giorgio Agamben, *Incoming*. London: Mack, 2017.

Mulvey, Laura, 'Visual pleasure and narrative cinema', *Screen* 16/3 (1975): 6–18; https://doi.org/10.1093/screen/16.3.6.

Mungwini, Pascah, '"Surveillance and cultural panopticism": situating Foucault in African modernities', *South African Journal of Philosophy* 31/2 (2012): 340–53; https://doi.org/10.1080/025801 36.2012.10751780.

Najmabadi, Afsaneh, 'Reading – and enjoying – "wiles of women" stories as a feminist', *Iranian Studies* 32/2 (1999): 203–22; https://doi.org/10.1080/00210869908701952.

Näsi, Matti, Maiju Tanskanen, Janne Kivivuori, Paula Haara and Esa Reunanen, 'Crime news consumption and fear of violence: the role of traditional media, social media, and alternative information sources', *Crime & Delinquency* 67/4 (2021): 574–600; https://doi.org/10.1177/0011128720922539.

Noble, Safiya Umoja, *Algorithms of Oppression: How Search Engines Reinforce Racism*. New York: New York University Press, 2018.

Nowicki, Jerry, 'State police tout 20 arrests, new tech in highway shootings', *Wednesday Journal of Oak Park and River Forest*, 8 February 2022; www.oakpark.com/2022/02/08/state-police-tout-20-arrests-new-tech-in-highway-shootings/.

Nwafor, Okechukwu C., 'Photography: Daguerreotype and the African experience', *Mgbakoigba: Journal of African Studies* 4 (2015): 11.

Paglen, Trevor, 'Operational images', *E-Flux Journal* no. 59 (2014); www.e-flux.com/journal/59/61130/operational-images/.

Pan, Xiuxi, Tomoya Nakamura, Xiao Chen and Masahiro Yamaguchi, 'Lensless inference camera: incoherent object recognition through a thin mask with LBP map generation', *Optics Express* 29/7 (2021): 9758; https://doi.org/10.1364/OE.416613.

Pearlman, Karen, and Adelheid Heftberger, 'Editorial: recognising women's work as creative work', *Apparatus: Film, Media and Digital Cultures in Central and Eastern Europe*, no. 6 (2018); www.apparatusjournal.net/index.php/apparatus/article/view/124/276.

Peterman, William, 'Our history', Oak Park Regional Housing Center; https://oprhc.org/regional_housing_center_history/.

Peters, John Durham, *The Marvelous Clouds: Toward a Philosophy of Elemental Media*. Chicago: University of Chicago Press, 2015.

Pew Research Center, 'Americans' trust in scientists, other groups declines', 15 February 2022; www.pewresearch.org/science/2022/02/15/americans-trust-in-scientists-other-groups-declines/.

———. 'Increasing public criticism, confusion over COVID-19 response in U.S.', February 2022; www.pewresearch.org/science/2022/02/09/increasing-public-criticism-confusion-over-covid-19-response-in-u-s/.

Picard, Sara, 'Racing Jules Lion', *Louisiana History: The Journal of the Louisiana Historical Association* 58/1 (2017): 5–37.

Pierce, James, 'Smart home security cameras and shifting lines of creepiness: a design-led inquiry', in *Proceedings of the 2019 CHI Conference on Human Factors in Computing Systems*; https://doi.org/10.1145/3290605.3300275.

Piza, Eric L., Brandon C. Welsh, David P. Farrington and Amanda L. Thomas, 'CCTV surveillance for crime prevention: a 40-year systematic review with meta-analysis', *Criminology & Public Policy* 18/1 (2019): 135–59; https://doi.org/10.1111/1745-9133.12419.

Postman, Neil, 'The reformed English curriculum', in *High School 1980: The Shape of the Future in American Secondary Education*, ed. Alvin C. Eurich. New York: Pitman, 1970, pp. 160–8.

Powers, Richard, *The Overstory: A Novel*. New York: W. W. Norton, 2018.

Qiu, Jack Linchuan, *Goodbye ISlave: A Manifesto for Digital Abolition*. Urbana: University of Illinois Press, 2016.

Raji, Inioluwa Deborah, and Joy Buolamwini, 'Actionable auditing: investigating the impact of publicly naming biased performance results of commercial AI products', in *Proceedings of the 2019 AAAI/ACM Conference on AI, Ethics, and Society*: 429–35; https://doi.org/10.1145/3306618.3314244.

Ramesh, Aditya, Mikhail Pavlov, Gabriel Goh, Scott Gray, Chelsea Voss, Alec Radford, Mark Chen and Ilya Sutskever, 'Zero-shot text-to-image generation', *arXiv* (2021); http://arxiv.org/abs/2102.12092.

Ratcliffe, Jerry H., Matthew Lattanzio, George Kikuchi and Kevin Thomas, 'A partially randomized field experiment on the effect of an acoustic gunshot detection system on police incident reports', *Journal of Experimental Criminology* 15/1 (2019): 67–76; https://doi.org/10.1007/s11292-018-9339-1.

Rettberg, Jill Walker, 'Apps as companions: how quantified self apps become our audience and our companions', in *Self-Tracking: Empirical and Philosophical Investigations*, ed. Btihaj Ajana. Basingstoke: Palgrave Macmillan, 2018, pp. 27–42; https://doi.org/10.1007/978-3-319-65379-2_3.

————. 'Et algoritmisk blikk: algoritmers rolle i produksjonen av hverdagsfotografier' [Seeing through algorithms: the algorithmic production of everyday photographs], *Norsk medietidsskrift* 26/01 (2019): 1–20; https://doi.org/10.18261/ISSN.0805-9535-2019-01 -03.

————. '"Nobody is ever alone": the use of social media narrative to include the viewer in SKAM', *Journal of Popular Culture* 54/2 (2021): 232–56; https://doi.org/10.1111/jpcu.13015.

————. *Seeing Ourselves through Technology: How We Use Selfies, Blogs and Wearable Devices to See and Shape Ourselves*. Basingstoke: Palgrave, 2014.

————. 'Situated data analysis: a new method for analysing encoded power relationships in social media platforms and apps', *Humanities and Social Sciences Communications* 7/1 (2020); https://doi.org/10.1057/s41599-020-0495-3.

————. 'Snapchat research stories', *Hyperrhiz: New Media Cultures* no. 21 (2019); https://doi.org/10.20415/hyp/021.m01.

————. 'Ways of knowing with data visualizations', in *Data Visualization in Society*, ed. Martin Engebretsen and Helen Kennedy. Amsterdam: Amsterdam University Press, 2020, pp. 35–47; https://doi.org/10.2307/j.ctvzgb8c7.

Rettberg, Jill Walker, Linda Kronman, Ragnhild Solberg, Marianne Gunderson, Stein Magne Bjørklund, Linn Heidi Stokkedal, Gabriele de Seta, Kurdin Jacob and Annette Markham, 'Representations of machine vision technologies in artworks, games and narratives: documentation of a dataset', *Data in Brief* 42 (2022); https://doi.org/10.1016/j.dib.2022.108319.

Rheingold, Howard, *Smart Mobs: The Next Social Revolution*. Cambridge, MA: Perseus Books, 2002.

Rodin, Auguste, and Paul Gsell, *Rodin on Art and Artists*, trans. Fedden Romily. New York: Dover, 1983.

Rogalski, A., 'History of infrared detectors', *Opto-Electronics Review* 20/3 (2012): 279–308; https://doi.org/10.2478/s11772-012-0037-7.

Roland, Alex, 'Once more into the stirrups: Lynn White Jr., medieval technology and social change',

Technology and Culture 44/3 (2003): 574–85; https://doi.org/10.1353/tech.2003.0131.

Rosenblatt, F., 'The perceptron: a probabilistic model for information storage and organization in the brain', *Psychological Review* 65/6 (1958): 386–408; https://doi.org/10.1037/h0042519.

———. 'The perceptron: a perceiving and recognizing automaton'. Technical Report 85-460-1. Ithaca, NY: Cornell Aeronautical Laboratory, January 1957.

St John, Nicola, 'Australian communication design history: an indigenous retelling', *Journal of Design History* 31/3 (2018): 255–73; https://doi.org/10.1093/jdh/epy014.

Saugmann, Rune, Frank Möller and Rasmus Bellmer, 'Seeing like a surveillance agency? Sensor realism as aesthetic critique of visual data governance', *Information, Communication & Society* 23/14 (2020): 1996–2013; https://doi.org/10.1080/1369118X.2020.1770315.

Sawyer, P. H., and R. H. Hilton, 'Technical determinism: the stirrup and the plough', *Past & Present*, no. 24 (1963): 90–100.

Schmidt-Burkhardt, Astrit, 'The all-seer: God's eye as proto-surveillance', in *Ctrl [space]: Rhetorics of Surveillance from Bentham to Big Brother*, ed. Peter Weibel, Ursula Frohne and Thomas Y. Levin. Cambridge, MA: MIT Press, 2002, pp. 17–32.

Seltzer, William, and Margo Anderson, 'The dark side of numbers: the role of population data systems in human rights abuses', *Social Research* 68/2 (2001): 481–513.

Selwyn, Neil, Liz Campbell and Mark Andrejevic, 'Autoroll: scripting the emergence of classroom facial recognition technology', *Learning, Media and Technology* 48/1 (2023): 166–79; https://doi.org/10.1080/17439884.2022.2039938.

Seneca, Lucius Annaeus, *Natural Questions*. Chicago: University of Chicago Press, 2010.

Shanthamallu, Uday Shankar, and Andreas Spanias, 'Introduction to machine learning', in Shanthamallu and Spanias, *Machine and Deep Learning Algorithms and Applications*. Cham: Springer International, 2022, pp. 1–8; https://doi.org/10.1007/978-3-031-03758-0_1.

Shklovsky, Victor, 'Art as technique', in *Modern Criticism and Theory*, ed. David Lodge. London: Longman, 1988, pp. 15–30.

Silver, Roxane Cohen, E. Alison Holman and Dana Rose Garfin, 'Coping with cascading collective traumas in the United States', *Nature Human Behaviour* 5/1 (2021): 4–6; https://doi.org/10.10 38/s41562-020-00981-x.

Simonite, Tom, 'AI license plate readers are cheaper – so drive carefully', *Wired*, 20 January 2020; www.wired.com/story/ai-license-pl ate-readers-cheaper-drive-carefully/.

Sines, George, and Yannis A. Sakellarakis, 'Lenses in antiquity', *American Journal of Archaeology* 91/2 (1987): 191; https://doi.org /10.2307/505216.

Sivin, Nathan, 'Review of *The Mozi: A Complete Translation (Translations from the Asian Classics)*, by Ian Johnston', *East Asian Science, Technology, and Medicine*, no. 32 (2012): 239–46.

Søbye, Espen, 'Et mørkt kapittel i statistikkens historie?', *Samfunnsspeilet*, no. 4 (1998): 2–17.

Solberg, Ragnhild, '(Always) playing the camera: cyborg vision and embodied surveillance in digital games', *Surveillance & Society* 20/2 (2022): 142–56.

———. 'Hologrammer i grenseland: ikke-menneskelige aktørers tilstedeværelse og handlingsrom i spill [Holograms in the borderlands: non-human presence and agency in games]', *Norsk Medietidsskrift* 28/4 (2021): 1–20; https://doi.org/10.18261/issn.0805-9535-2021 -04-03.

———. '"Too easy" or "too much"? (Re)imagining protagonistic empowerment through machine vision in video games', *Przegląd Kulturoznawczy (Arts & Cultural Studies Review)* issue 4 (no. 54) (2022).

Sontag, Susan, *On Photography*. New York: Picador, 1977.

Stubblefield, Thomas, *Drone Art: The Everywhere War as Medium*. Oakland: University of California Press, 2020.

Strate, Lance, *Media Ecology: An Approach to Understanding the Human Condition*. New York: Peter Lang, 2017.

Szegedy, Christian, Wojciech Zaremba, Ilya Sutskever, Joan Bruna, Dumitru Erhan, Ian Goodfellow and Rob Fergus, 'Intriguing properties of neural networks', arXiv (2013); https://doi.org/10.48550/ARXIV.1312.6199.

Taffel, Sy, *Digital Media Ecologies: Entanglements of Content, Code and Hardware*. New York: Bloomsbury Academic, 2019.

Thomee, Bart, David A. Shamma, Gerald Friedland, Benjamin Elizalde, Karl Ni, Douglas Poland, Damian Borth and Li-Jia Li, 'YFCC100M: the new data in multimedia research', *Communications of the ACM* 59/2 (2016): 64–73; https://doi.org/10.1145/2812802.

Thompson, Kristin, 'Government policies and practical necessities in the Soviet cinema of the 1920s', in *The Red Screen: Politics, Society, Art in Soviet Cinema*, ed. Anna Lawton. New York: Routledge, 1992, pp. 19–42.

Tomasello, Michael, Brian Hare, Hagen Lehmann and Josep Call, 'Reliance on head versus eyes in the gaze following of great apes and human infants: the cooperative eye hypothesis', *Journal of Human Evolution* 52/3 (2007): 314–20; https://doi.org/10.1016/j.jhevol.2006.10.001.

Tovey, Rob, 'Photomaps: a visual taxonomy', *Visual Communication* 17/2 (2018): 209–20; https://doi.org/10.1177/1470357217746028.

Tseng, Ethan, Shane Colburn, James Whitehead, Luocheng Huang, Seung-Hwan Baek, Arka Majumdar and Felix Heide, 'Neural nano-optics for high-quality thin lens imaging', *Nature Communications* 12/1 (2021): 6493; https://doi.org/10.1038/s41467-021-26443-0.

Tsing, Anna Lowenhaupt, *The Mushroom at the End of the World: On the Possibility of Life in Capitalist Ruins*. Princeton, NJ: Princeton University Press, 2017.

Uricchio, William, 'The algorithmic turn: photosynth, augmented reality and the changing implications of the image', *Visual Studies* 26/1 (2011): 25–35; https://doi.org/10.1080/1472586X.2011.548486.

Van der Nagel, Emily, '"Networks that work too well": intervening in algorithmic connections', *Media International Australia* 168/1 (2018): 81–92; https://doi.org/10.1177/1329878X18783002.

Van Noorden, Richard, 'The ethical questions that haunt facial-recognition research', *Nature* 587 (November 2020): 354–8.

Vertov, Dziga, *Kino-Eye: The Writings of Dziga Vertov*, ed. Annette Michelson, trans. Kevin O'Brian. Berkeley: University of California Press, 1984.

Village of Oak Park, 'Meeting minutes, village board meeting March 21, 2022'; https://t.co/Av6limyrJj.

Virilio, Paul, *The Vision Machine*, trans. Julie Rose. Bloomington: University of Indiana Press, 1994.

Wachter-Boettcher, Sara, *Technically Wrong: Sexist Apps, Biased Algorithms, and Other Threats of Toxic Tech*. New York: W. W. Norton, 2017.

White, Jacob, and Felipe Yamashita, '*Boquila trifoliolata* mimics leaves of an artificial plastic host plant', *Plant Signaling & Behavior* 17/1 (2022); https://doi.org/10.1080/15592324.2021.1977530.

White, Lynn, *Medieval Technology and Social Change*. Oxford: Oxford University Press, 1962.

Willis, Deborah, *Reflections in Black: A History of Black Photographers 1840 to the Present*. New York: W. W. Norton, 2000.

Winner, Langdon, 'Do artifacts have politics?' *Daedalus* 109/1 (1980): 121–36.

Yong, Ed, *An Immense World: How Animal Senses Reveal the Hidden Realms around Us*. New York: Random House, 2022.

Ytre-Arne, Brita, and Hallvard Moe, 'Folk theories of algorithms: understanding digital irritation', *Media, Culture & Society* 43/5 (2021): 807–24; https://doi.org/10.1177/0163443720972314.

Referenced artworks, games and stories

Anadol, Refik, *Machine Hallucination*, 2019; https://refikanadol.com/works/machine-hallucination/ [exhibition and performance; documentation].

Atwood, Margaret, *The Handmaid's Tale*. Toronto: McClelland & Stewart, 1985 [novel].

Brooker, Charlie, *Black Mirror*. Channel 4 and Netflix, 2011–19 [TV series].

Collins, Suzanne, *The Hunger Games*. New York: Scholastic Press, 2008 [novel; the sequels and movies are also briefly mentioned].

Dewey-Hagborg, Heather, *Radical Love: Chelsea Manning*, 2016; https://deweyhagborg.com/projects/radical-love [art installation; documentation].

Doctorow, Cory, *Little Brother*. New York: Tor Books, 2008 [novel].

Elwes, Jake, *Zizi – Queering the Dataset*, 2019; www.jakeelwes.com/project-zizi-2019.html [video artwork; documentation].

Harvey, Adam, *CV Dazzle*, 2010; https://ahprojects.com/cvdazzle [artwork; documentation].

Kronman, Linda, and Andreas Zingerle, *Suspicious Behavior*, 2020; https://kairus.org/portfolio/suspicious-behavior-2020/ [interactive digital art; documentation].

McCarthy, Lauren Lee, and Kyle McDonald, *US+*; https://lauren-mccarthy.com/us [interactive artwork; documentation].

McEwan, Ian, *Machines Like Me*. London: Jonathan Cape, 2019 [novel].

Monáe, Janelle, 2018. *Dirty Computer*, 2018; https://youtu.be/jdH2Sy-BlNE [album and 'emotion picture' video; see also the collection of short stories set in this fictional world by Janelle Monáe and collaborators].

Monty Python, 'How not to be seen' *Monty Python's Flying Circus*, episode 24. BBC, 1969.

Mosse, Richard, *Incoming*, 2014–17 [exhibited as a series of photos and as video; a book version was published by Mack in London in 2019].

Niantic, *Pokemon Go*, 2016 [mobile video game].

Okorafor, Nnedi, *Lagoon*. New York: Simon & Schuster, 2014 [novel].

Orwell, George, *Nineteen Eighty-Four*. London: Secker & Warburg, 1949 [novel].

Paglen, Trevor, and Kate Crawford, *ImageNet Roulette*, 2020; https://paglen.studio/2020/04/29/imagenet-roulette/ [artwork; documentation].

Peng! Collective, *Mask.ID*, 2018; https://pen.gg/campaign/mask-id -2/ [artwork; documentation].

Powers, Richard, *The Overstory*. New York: W. W. Norton, 2018 [novel].

Shusterman, Neal, *Thunderhead*, Vol. 2 of *Arc of a Scythe*. New York: Simon & Schuster, 2018 [novel].

Steyerl, Hito, *How Not to be Seen: A Fucking Didactic Educational .mov File*, 2013; www.moma.org/learn/moma_learning/hito-ste yerl-how-not-to-be-seen-a-fucking-didactic-educational-mov-fi le-2013/ [video artwork; in MoMA's online collection].

Sony Interactive Entertainment, *Detroit: Become Human*, Playstation 4, 2018 [video game].

Spielberg, Steven, *Minority Report*. 20th Century Fox, 2002 [film; loosely based on a short story by Philip K. Dick].

Ubisoft, *Watch Dogs*, 2014–20 [video game series].

Zer-Aviv, Mushon. 2012. *The Normalizing Machine*, 2012; https://mushon.com/tnm/ [interactive art installation; documentation].

Note

For more examples of art, games, movies and novels about machine vision, see the Database of Machine Vision in Art, Games and Narratives at https://machinevisionuib.github.io. This documents 500 creative works (including 77 digital games, 190 digital artworks and 233 movies, novels and other narratives) that use or represent machine vision technologies. The data can also be downloaded as a set of csv files for reuse or analysis. A paper authored by Rettberg et al. documenting this dataset, with a link to the downloadable files, is listed in the references.

Index

References to figures are in *italics*.